G. Washington

THE TAPPAN-KENDALL HISTORIES

AMERICAN HERO STORIES

BY

EVA MARCH TAPPAN, Ph.D.

Author of " England's Story," " An Elementary History of
Our Country," " Our European Ancestors," etc.

Fredonia Books
Amsterdam, The Netherlands

American Hero Stories

by
Eva March Tappan

ISBN: 1-58963-342-3

Reprinted from the 1920 edition

Fredonia Books
Amsterdam, The Netherlands
http://www.fredoniabooks.com

In order to make original editions of historical works
available to scholars at an economical price, this
facsimile of the original edition of 1920 is
reproduced from the best available copy and has
been digitally enhanced to improve legibility, but the
text remains unaltered to retain historical
authenticity.

PREFACE

IF I were teaching the history of the United States to boys and girls of nine or ten, I would do it by having them read simple, picturesque stories of the men who have made our country what it is. Then I would let the children talk of what they had read and ask questions about it. Some of these questions I would answer; some I would ask them to try to answer for themselves. I would say nothing about exact dates, but I would make four or five general divisions of our history, such as discoveries and settlements, Colonial days and Indian wars, the Revolution, and so on. I would go through the stories rapidly in their chronological order, bringing out any information that the children might have gathered and occasionally adding a word to connect the stories or to make some point clear.

What would this accomplish? At the end of the reading the children would be on good terms with twenty-five or more of the chief actors in the story of the United States; they would be well prepared for a "real history," and, best of all, they would look forward to it, not with dread, but with pleasant anticipation.

This book is written from this viewpoint. It contains five accounts of voyages and explorers, ranging from Columbus to Lewis and Clark; stories of five colonies of marked dissimilarity — Virginia, Quebec, Plymouth, New York, and Philadelphia; brief lives of four pioneers of the eighteenth and nineteenth centuries; fifteen short stories of war time; and a sketch of Roosevelt's career. In treating of our wars, it seemed wisest not to attempt any formal explanation of causes and results, but rather to picture a number

PREFACE

of separate and interesting achievements, choosing as far as possible actions that have distinct heroes. The chapters are arranged in chronological order, with a thread of continuity running through them. The aim of the book is to introduce in informal and friendly fashion some of the makers of American history, and to provide a simple, broad foundation for future study of history and biography.

Acknowledgments are due to the courtesy of the following for permission to use their material for illustrations: to The Title Guarantee and Trust Co. of New York for *New Amsterdam in Stuyvesant's Time;* to Mr. C. M. Barton, President of the Historical Society of Michigan, for *Gladwyn's Warning from the Indian Girl;* to Mr. Charles E. Goodspeed for *Washington at the Delaware;* to McClure's Magazine for portrait of *Daniel Boone;* to the New England Magazine for *The Indian Woman who Guided Lewis and Clark* and the *Seal of the Lewis and Clark Exposition;* to The Outing Magazine for *The Marriage* and *The March of David Crockett.* The illustrations in the chapter on Roosevelt are from photographs copyrighted by Underwood and Underwood, and by W. S. Ritch.

EVA MARCH TAPPAN.

WORCESTER, MASSACHUSETTS,
March 18, 1920.

CONTENTS

CONTENTS

CHRISTOPHER COLUMBUS

WHO FIRST CROSSED THE ATLANTIC OCEAN

A LITTLE boy once lived in Genoa, Italy, whose earliest memory was the " Boom, boom ! " of his father's shuttle. The father was a wool comber and weaver, and all the near neighbors were weavers. When the boy went to school he studied and played with the children of weavers; and when he went to church he knelt before an altar that belonged specially to the weavers. He would probably have become a weaver himself if Genoa had not been a seashore town. The wharves were not far from his home; and even when he went to walk on the hills back of the city, he could not help seeing the white-sailed ships coming and going. When he was fourteen, he sailed away on one of them, and for fourteen years he went on one voyage after another. Between the voyages he helped his father comb wool and weave.

Genoa was full of sailor boys. No one knew that this boy would become a famous man, and so no one wrote any account of his boyhood. Almost the only thing we know about his early years is that he managed somehow to learn a great many things. He learned how to sail a ship by watching the moon and stars and using the instruments that sailors then had. He learned all that was known about geography. He learned to draw beautiful maps and sea-charts. Some of these maps were different from those of to-day. When he drew a map of Europe, for instance, he put the Atlantic Ocean west of the Continent, and Asia west of the Atlantic. Europe in those days was buying spices, silks, and many other things from China and eastern Asia; but bringing them overland by caravans was very expensive. "Why cannot we cross the Atlantic," Columbus said to himself, "and so go directly to China?"

There were several reasons why people thought this could not be done. A few believed that the earth was a sphere and could be sailed around. But some said the Atlantic was full of monsters and demons, and others thought that the water at the equator was boiling hot. Columbus was not troubled by any of these fears, but he had no money to provide ships and men for such a voyage. In those days Portugal was a great sea power, so he appealed to the Portuguese king. "If you will give me ships and men," he said, "I will cross the Atlantic. Then you can trade directly with the great cities of China and Japan, and Portugal will become the richest country in Europe." He gave all his reasons for believing that this could be done, and King John agreed to lay the matter before four learned men. These men replied, "It is a wild and foolish scheme." But one of them added, "If there is any truth in it, why should we let this foreigner have all the glory? Let us

CARAVEL OF THE TIME OF COLUMBUS
From the Latin letter of Columbus printed in 1493

keep him waiting awhile and send out one of our own sailors." So a ship was sent out secretly; but a storm arose, and in a few days it came back. "No one can ever cross the Atlantic," declared the frightened captain.

Columbus heard of the trick and was indignant. "I will go to the sovereigns of Spain," he said to himself; and he set off on foot to cross the mountains. Some time before this he had married, and his wife had died, leaving him a little boy, Diego, who was now about six years old. Diego walked until he was tired, then his father carried him, and so they journeyed into Spain. Diego was left with his aunt, and Columbus made an appeal to King Ferdinand and Queen Isabella. The queen liked Columbus and was interested in his plans; but when she asked the opinion of her learned councilors, they said, as the council in Portugal had said, "It is a wild and foolish scheme." The queen was not convinced, but the kingdom was at war and there was little money to spare for expeditions. So, after seven years of waiting, Columbus took Diego and set off for France.

Before they had walked far, the boy was hungry, and his father rang the bell of the convent of La Rábida. "Will you give me some bread for my son?" he asked. "Yes, surely," replied the monks. "Bring the boy in and let him rest." One of these monks, called Brother Antonio, noticed that Columbus was no common beggar, and they had a long talk together. Brother Antonio was almost as much interested in geography and astronomy as Columbus himself, and soon Columbus had told him his plans for crossing the ocean and all his disappointments. The prior of the convent also became interested. "Do not go to France yet," he said. " Before I came here, I was confessor to the queen. I will write to her, and perhaps she will listen to me." She did listen; and before many days had passed, the little seaport town of Palos was in a fever of excitement, for three ships were to sail from there to cross the Atlantic, the " Sea of Darkness," as it was called.

One bright morning in August, 1492, the ships sailed. " They will never come back again," said the wise people on the shore; and it was not long before the sailors were ready to agree with them, for the needle of the compass no longer pointed to the north. Then the ships began to pass great masses of floating seaweed. " It will grow thicker and thicker," said the sailors, " and we shall never get out of it." Columbus explained these wonders as well as he could, but soon there was more trouble. " The wind always blows from the east," declared the men, " and we shall never be able to get home again." Fortunately the wind changed one day and blew from the west. Day after day passed, and still no land was seen. The men began to gather in little groups and to whisper together. " There is no land here," they said. " The admiral is crazy. Let us throw him overboard and go home before our provisions give out." Columbus learned what they were saying. He

called them up before him and said, " The sovereigns
of Spain have sent me to find the Indies, and with the
help of God I will go on until I see them." The very
next morning a green rush floated by, and a stick that
had been cut was picked up. Then the branch of some
tree with red berries on it was seen. The men forgot
their fears and were as eager as the admiral himself to
hasten on.

Night came, but Columbus could not sleep. He stood
gazing earnestly into the west, and suddenly he saw a
light that moved as if some one was walking and carrying a torch. When the moon rose, it shone on the white
sand of one of the islands that are now called the
Bahamas.

In the morning Columbus put on his richest uniform,
all aglow with scarlet and gold, and was rowed ashore.
He fell on his knees, kissed the ground, and thanked
God for his goodness. Then he unfurled the royal
standard and cried, " In the name of the glorious sovereigns, Ferdinand and Isabella, I take possession of
this land and name it San Salvador."

All this time a crowd of people, half hidden in the
woods, were watching Columbus and his men with wide-
open eyes. At first they were frightened; but when
they saw that the strangers did not attempt to harm
them, they came nearer and nearer. " Those are good
spirits come down from the skies," they whispered.

MASS UPON COLUMBUS'S ARRIVAL.

From a Latin history of Columbus's voyages published in 1621

They threw themselves on their knees before the Spaniards to show their reverence. Then they touched the clothes and beards and white skins of the explorers, and welcomed them as well as they could by signs. Columbus gave them glass beads and little bells and red and blue caps, and they brought him in return tame parrots, baskets of fruit, and great balls of cotton yarn.

These natives were copper colored. Their hair was straight and black and they had no beards. They were naked, unless the rings that some of them wore in their noses could be called articles of dress. The Spaniards looked eagerly at these rings, for they seemed to be of pure gold. "Where does the gold come from?" they asked as well as they could by signs. "Over there," the natives replied, pointing to the southwest. Columbus supposed that he was on one of the islands off eastern Asia, and that they were pointing to the mainland. For many weeks he sailed among the islands, hoping to find some of the great cities of Asia. Then he decided to go home and report to the sovereigns. "I can come again next year," he thought. "Now that I have found the way to India, there will be no lack of ships or men."

More than two months later, the bells of Palos rang merrily, the shops and schools were closed, and the whole town flocked to the wharves, for Columbus was coming up the river. As soon as he had landed, a procession was formed, and he went to the church to thank

God for bringing him safely home. It is easy to guess where he went next, for Columbus never forgot those who had been kind to him. He went straight to his old friends, the monks of La Rabida. From there he sent a letter to the sovereigns.

Then there was great excitement at the Spanish court. The sovereigns wrote Columbus a letter, addressed to "Don Christopher Columbus, our admiral of the ocean sea, and viceroy and governor of the islands discovered in the Indies." This letter bade him come to court at once, and Columbus obeyed. All the way people lined the roads and stood at the doors and windows, gazing at the great man and cheering as he went by. When he reached Barcelona, a procession was formed. First came six Indians whom Columbus had brought with him. They were followed by the sailors carrying parrots, stuffed birds, the skins of strange beasts, plants, berries, and ornaments of gold that had come from the other side of the Atlantic. Then came the admiral on horseback in a handsome uniform, and after him a brilliant company of young nobles flashing with jewels.

When they reached the royal audience room, there sat the king and queen on their throne, with a glittering canopy of cloth of gold over their heads. Around them stood the courtiers and the proudest nobles of Spain, all watching to catch the first glimpse of the man who

had made the wonderful voyage. Among them must
have been the boy Diego, for the queen had made him
a page to her son.

Columbus walked slowly up the room, gray-haired,
dignified, as stately as any of the lordly Spaniards. He

COLUMBUS RECOUNTING HIS ADVENTURES AT COURT

knelt before the throne to kiss the hands of the sovereigns; but they rose as they would have risen to greet
any mighty king and bade him be seated. Then he
told them about the voyage, the new lands, and the
strange people whom he had seen. "There are even
greater discoveries before us," he said. "The wealth

of many kingdoms will come to Spain, and there are thousands of heathen to whom Spain can teach the religion of Christ."

The king and queen wished Columbus to make another voyage at once. He did not have to plead for help now, for they said, "Send us the list of what vessels, food, and arms you will need, and they shall be supplied." As for men, there were thousands who would have been glad to go with him, for people believed that whoever went on this voyage would make his fortune. Soon the fleet of seventeen vessels was ready, and crowds of people stood on the shore cheering as it sailed away.

It is almost a pity that the story of Columbus does not end here, for in the rest of his life there was much trouble and disappointment. He went on a third voyage, and this time he coasted along the continent of South America. He would have been glad to explore farther, but he had to go to Hayti to care for some colonists who had crossed the ocean with him on his second voyage. They had no idea of working for the wealth they expected to get. They were discontented and quarrelsome, and they blamed Columbus for all their troubles. Some of them returned to Spain, and there made such complaints of the admiral that an officer named Bobadilla was sent to Hayti to take his place. Bobadilla threw Columbus into chains and accused him

of so many crimes that he expected to be put to death
without even a hearing. The great man was taken on
board a vessel to be carried back to Spain. As soon
as they were away from Bobadilla, the captain and the
owner of the vessel knelt before the prisoner and began
to take off his irons. " No," said the admiral, " the king
and queen sent the man who put these chains upon me,
and they alone shall take them off."

All the way to Spain Columbus wore the fetters, but
he was treated with as much honor as could have been
shown to the king himself; and as soon as the sovereigns saw what wrong had been done him, they tried
to make amends. Still they were almost as much disappointed as the colonists, for they had expected that
Columbus would find the rich cities of Asia. Something had happened, too, while he was gone on this
voyage, that made them even more dissatisfied. A Portuguese named Vasco da Gama had discovered that it
was possible to sail around Africa; and he had returned
with loads of silks and satins, spices, ivory, emeralds,
and rubies. " That is the way to go to the Indies,"
declared the sea captains. " What is the use of trying
to get to Japan and China by crossing the Atlantic?"

Then Columbus determined to go on a fourth voyage.
He had no thought that a vast continent and the Pacific
Ocean lay between China and the islands that he had
seen. He believed that he could find a passage between

the islands which would lead from the Atlantic to the Indian Ocean. Of course no such passage could be found, and he had to return to Spain, where he died less than two years later. He had dreamed of being very rich; all his life he was poor. He had dreamed of finding the Indies; he had failed. He died a disappointed man; but if he could have looked ahead four hundred years and seen the America of to-day, he would surely have rejoiced that he was the discoverer, not of a shorter way to India, but of a mighty continent.

OUTLINE

Boyhood of Columbus — plan for crossing the Atlantic — supposed dangers of the voyage — appeal to Portugal — trickery of the Portuguese — journey to Spain — appeal to the Spanish sovereigns — La Rábida — Columbus sails at last — troubles of the voyage — signs of land — going ashore — the natives — the return to Spain — Columbus at court — second voyage — third voyage — the discontented colonists — Columbus in chains — Portuguese discoveries — fourth voyage — death.

SUGGESTIONS FOR WRITTEN WORK

Diego tells another boy of his journey from Portugal to Spain, and of his visit to La Rábida.

Columbus appeals to the Spanish sovereigns.

A sailor gives an account of Columbus's first voyage.

A native of San Salvador describes the coming of the Spaniards.

FERDINAND MAGELLAN

WHO FOUND THE WAY AROUND THE WORLD

WHILE Columbus was trying to persuade the Portuguese king to provide him with ships for crossing the "Sea of Darkness," a baby was born far up among the mountains of Portugal who was to become as great a sailor as the famous admiral himself. When this child, Ferdinand Magellan, became a man, he found himself living in exciting times. Now that Columbus had shown the way, others crossed the Atlantic. They explored various parts of the coast, and at last people began to realize that not a group of islands but a great mass of land lay between the Atlantic and China. They hoped to find a passage through it. Everybody was talking about voyages. From early in the morning till long after the sun had set, the hammers of the shipbuilders rang; and sometimes the last blow was hardly struck on a vessel before every place was taken, from captain to cabin boy.

Magellan served in the Portuguese navy faithfully for many years, but when he asked for the promotion that was his due, the king refused. "Will you give me permission to serve some other sovereign?" demanded Magellan. "Do what you like," the king replied coldly. Magellan knelt to kiss his hand, as was usual in parting.

but the king drew it back. The indignant sailor went straight to Spain and laid his plans before the Spanish ruler.

"I have been in the Indies for seven years," he said, "and I know what wealth one can get by buying spices of the natives. My friend Serrano is now in the Moluccas, and this is what he writes me." He showed the letter of Serrano in which was written, "Here is a new world. Come if you want to get rich." Then said Magellan, "If you will give me ships and men, I will go to the lands across the Atlantic, and I will follow the coast southward till I come to some strait that leads to the China Sea. I will find the way to the Moluccas, and I will bring home such loads of spices as never yet came into any Spanish port."

MAGELLAN

The king granted his request, and then came a busy time of making ready. The ships must carry provisions

for two years at least. They must have a good supply
of powder and shot and cannon balls of iron and of
stone. There must be darts and javelins and lances and
pikes and crossbows and arquebuses and coats of mail.
The natives of the Moluccas would not care for money,
but they would care for glass beads, fishhooks, and
bright-colored cloth, brass and copper bracelets, brass
basins, little bells, knives, scissors, and looking-glasses;
therefore a great quantity of these things was stored
in the holds of the vessels. There were twenty thousand
little bells, for instance, and five hundred pounds of
glass beads.

These treasures were useful long before the explorers
came to the Moluccas. Their first landing-place on this
side of the Atlantic was in the Bay of Rio de Janeiro,
and there the natives swarmed about the ships. "Give
me that," one would say by signs, "and you may have
this." The native would paddle away with a little bell
or a fishhook, and the sailors would hasten to cook the
big basketful of sweet potatoes or the half-dozen fowl
that he had given in exchange.

The ships kept close to the shore, and before long
they were at the mouth of the Rio de la Plata. "It is
possible that this is a strait," thought Magellan. For
two days he sailed up the stream, but the water became
fresher every hour, so he knew that he was in a river.
He turned back and went on to the south, gazing

closely at every opening that looked as if it might be a passage. The weather grew colder and colder; and at last he saw that he could go no farther before spring. So he anchored in a sheltered bay and shortened the rations. Then he had to meet greater trouble than ice and snow, for the sailors began to grumble. " There is no strait," they said. " This land stretches from pole to pole. Our lives are worth more than all the cloves of the Moluccas. Let us start for home."

Magellan, however, had no idea of giving up. " Of what do you complain?" he asked. "Here is a sheltered bay with plenty of wood. There are fish in its waters and there are birds on its shores. The winter will soon be past, and then we can push on to a world that is rich in gold and spices. Your king will not forget to reward you. Will you go back to Spain and say, 'We were cold, and so we came home'? You are Spaniards, and Spaniards are brave. _I_ would rather die than turn back!" After this talk the sailors were content, but the captains led them into a second rebellion. Then the admiral did not plead, but punished the leaders severely.

One morning an amazingly tall man appeared on the shore of the bay. He danced and sang and poured sand on his head. " Go ashore," said Magellan to one of his men. " Do whatever he does, and see if you can make friends with him." The sailor went ashore. When the giant danced, he danced; and when the giant poured sand on his head, the sailor poured sand on his own head. " Come on board our ship," said the sailor by signs, and the native went. He was so tall that it is said the Spaniards came up only to his waistband. They soon found that he was strong, for when they showed him his face in a little looking-glass, he was so amazed that he jumped backward with a force that threw four men down on the deck. Other natives almost as tall came afterwards. Their feet were dressed so clumsily that the Spaniards called them Patagonians, or large-

footed men. These giants were good-natured and gentle. The chaplain taught one of them to say the Lord's Prayer, and he was so pleased that he walked about shouting it at the top of his voice.

As soon as spring had come, the ships went on. Another opening showed itself. " It may be the strait we are look-

ONE OF MAGELLAN'S SHIPS
From a drawing of the sixteenth century

ing for," thought Magellan, and he sent two of his ships to explore. Suddenly a fierce storm broke out. Several days passed, but no ships appeared. " They are surely wrecked," said the sailors, gazing anxiously over the water. "What is that coming around the point?" one of them cried, for he had caught sight of a white sail shining in the sun. In a moment more the two lost ships were in view. All sails were set, and flags and pennons were fluttering in the wind. "Boom! Boom!" went the big guns. "Hurrah!" shouted the men on the lost vessels. "Hurrah!" shouted the men who had been waiting. "What have you found?" Magellan called eagerly. "Is it a bay?"

"It is a deep channel," they replied; "it is no bay and no river."

The admiral called his captains and pilots. "Shall we go on?" he asked.

"No!" replied one of the pilots. "We have not much food, and if there should be a storm or a calm for some time, we should starve. We have found the strait, and now let us go home and come back with another fleet."

"Do you all agree?" demanded Magellan.

"No!" cried the others. "Why should we go back now that the way has become easy! The Moluccas must be close at hand. Let us keep on."

"We will," declared Magellan quietly, and he would probably have said the same whether the others agreed or not; "we will go on till we have found the Moluccas. We will keep our promise to the king if we have to eat the leather on the ships' yards. May God help us and give us good fortune!"

On they went through the winding passage which was afterwards known as the Strait of Magellan; and at last there came a day when the stern commander wept for joy, for before him spread a broad ocean so calm and quiet that he called it the Pacific.

Now the navigators of that day made one great mistake: they thought the earth was much smaller than it is. Magellan supposed that he was perhaps a two or three weeks' sail from the Moluccas; but he went on and on, and still they seemed to come no nearer. There were provisions for only three months, and two months had already passed. "Land ahead!" cried the watch one day, and then every one was happy. But the land proved to be only a little island with no water, no fruit, no food of any kind. It was too late to turn back, for they had not provisions enough for the voyage across the Atlantic; so they spread all sail and went onward, watching the western horizon as closely as Columbus had done. The little water that was left on board was so brackish that, thirsty as they were, they could hardly drink it. The biscuits were stale. At last even these gave out, and the men really did eat the leather on the ships' yards. They were almost ready to eat the ships themselves.

After fourteen weeks of suffering on the Pacific, it was rather hard that, when they did come to land, they should fall among thieves. But so it was. They anchored off a group of islands to buy food, and the natives swarmed over the vessels and stole from under the owners' very eyes everything they could lay their hands upon. They did not spare even the admiral, for they stole the small boat which hung at the stern of his ship. It is no wonder that he named the islands Ladrones, or the thieves' islands.

Then came another group of islands which long afterwards were called Philippines; and now the sailors had plenty of oranges, cocoanuts, and " figs a foot long," as they called bananas.

" Where is the best place to buy spices? " Magellan asked the chief.

" Over at the island of Sebu," he replied.

" Will you give us guides to show us the way? "

" If you will help me get my rice in, I myself will show you," was the reply. So the proud Spaniards went out among the rice and worked two days to help a savage chief bring in his crop. Then they all sailed to Sebu.

The king of Sebu was very friendly. " You shall be my brother," he said to Magellan, " and no one but Spaniards shall trade in my land." They made a formal treaty of friendship. " I will help you to punish those who do not obey you," said Magellan. The chief of the little island of Mactan had no idea of obeying the king

of Sebu, and Magellan set out to punish him. " Do not
do it," pleaded the admiral's friends. " It is no gain to
us if we conquer them." He would not yield, however,
for the friendliness of the king of Sebu had given him
an idea which he meant to carry out. " What a glorious
thing it would be," he had said to himself, " if I could
report to the king of Spain that all these islands are willing to obey him and to trade with no other countries ! "
He made ready for what he thought would be only a little
skirmish. It never entered his mind that forty-nine men
in armor could be overpowered by any number of savages; so the Spaniards rowed boldly up to the island and
landed. They were greeted with a storm of arrows and
spears; but where were the islanders ? Safely hidden in
the bushes. Not one Spanish shot in twenty did them any
harm. Of course they tried hardest to kill Magellan.
He was wounded many times; but he held out for a
long while, hoping to give his men time to retreat. At
last he fell. One of the men who kept close by his side
wrote afterwards, " The Indians threw themselves upon
him with iron-pointed bamboo spears and scimitars and
every weapon they had, and ran him through until they
killed him." The Spaniards retreated to their ships.
That night they sent a messenger to beg for the admiral's body. " Give it to us and you shall have cloth,
bells, knives, whatever you like," he said. But the savages replied, " No, not for the whole world. We shall

keep that body, and then we can say to our enemies,
' See what we took from the lordly Spaniards ! ' "

There was nothing to do but to press on to the
Moluccas, and before long the vessels were off the little
island of Tidor. The chief came on board for a friendly
call. He was not an altogether easy visitor to entertain,
for, as he would never bow his head, it was rather difficult to get him safely into the little cabin. He and the
Spaniards agreed on how much should be paid for cloves.
Red cloth, yellow cloth, linen, hatchets, knives, scissors,
and caps were to be given in generous quantities; but
soon there were so many cloves to be sold and so few to
buy them that a yard of bright-colored ribbon would pay
for one hundred pounds of the precious spice. Every
sailor was allowed to carry home a certain number of
pounds. All were eager to buy, and when their trinkets
gave out, they bartered even their jackets and shirts;
so they were somewhat scantily clad when they sailed
homeward.

Five vessels had left Spain. One was lost off the coast
of Patagonia; one proved unseaworthy and was burned;
one deserted and returned to Spain; one finally fell into
the hands of the Portuguese; and the Victoria alone
was left. As she crossed the Indian Ocean and rounded
the Cape of Good Hope, the air must have been fragrant
behind her, for, besides all that the officers and sailors
bought for themselves, she carried twenty-six tons of

cloves. In 1522, three years from the time that the
Victoria sailed away, she anchored near Seville. Magellan was gone; but it was he who planned the voyage,
and it was his courage and perseverance that made it
possible. His body remained in far-away Mactan, but
the glory of the first journey around the world is his
alone.

OUTLINE

What was known of the western lands in Magellan's day —
Magellan's request of the king of Portugal — his appeal to the king
of Spain — preparations for the voyage — barter with the South
Americans — up the Rio de la Plata — discontent of the sailors —
discovery of the Strait of Magellan — crossing the Pacific — the
Ladrones — the Philippines — the alliance with the king of Sebu
— the fight at Mactan — death of Magellan — buying cloves — the
homeward voyage.

SUGGESTIONS FOR WRITTEN WORK

A boy tells his father why he wishes to sail with Magellan.
A sailor describes the meeting with the Patagonians.
A sailor tells his friends at home of buying cloves at Tidor.

FRANCIS DRAKE

SEAMAN OF QUEEN ELIZABETH

WITHIN fifty years after Columbus had shown the
way to America, Spaniards, Italians, English,
French, and Portuguese visited the New World. All
were hoping to find gold; but the Spaniards were most

successful, for they con-
quered Mexico and
Peru, and won their rich
mines of gold and silver.
Every year ships loaded
with American treasure
sailed into Spanish ports.
England and Spain were
not on good terms, and
it was the special delight
of the English seamen to
capture a treasure ship.
One of the most daring
of these seamen was
named Francis Drake.

Even when Drake was
a very small boy, he
wanted to go to sea. If
there had been no one to
object, he could almost

FRANCIS DRAKE

From an original portrait in St. James's
Palace

have launched his own house and sailed away on the
ocean, for he, his parents, and a troop of younger
brothers lived in the hulk of a great war-ship that lay
just off the queen's dockyard in Chatham. When he
awoke in the early morning, he could hear the little waves
beating against the sides of the vessel. Then as he lay
and listened, the sound of hammers could be heard, the

creaking of ropes, and the songs of the workmen in the dockyard. Strange, wild dreams had this little blue-eyed boy. " Some day," he said to himself, " I will go off on one of those boats that the men are building. I will fight with the Spaniards, and I will capture great ships loaded with silver and gold. Then when I come sailing back to Plymouth, the people on the wharf will shout, ' Three cheers for Francis Drake ! ' "

With his mind full of such dreams as these, he must have felt disappointed when he was sent to sea with the skipper of a small trading vessel. There was no hope of capturing Spanish ships, for the little craft did nothing but sail quietly back and forth between England and Holland or France, carrying goods to sell in the different markets. Still he was at least on the ocean; so he made the best of it, and worked so faithfully that when the skipper died, he gave the young sailor the boat. Drake might have gone on trading if Spain and England had been friends; but Spain had begun to send out vessels to seize every English craft that could be captured, and Francis Drake's little coaster would have stood small chance of escape. So he sold it, and went on several voyages on vessels that were larger and better able to protect themselves.

On one of these voyages he sailed away in the highest spirits. " When I come back, I shall be a rich man," he said to himself. There were six vessels in the little

squadron. The admiral was a famous sailor, Sir John
Hawkins. Drake was put in command of the Judith.
They sailed to the African coast, seized some negroes,
carried them to the Spanish settlements, and sold them
as slaves. The ships were loaded with the gold and
pearls which had been received in payment, and started
for England. Before they had sailed many days, they
were so disabled by a storm that the admiral had to put
into the Spanish port of Vera Cruz for repairs. There,
in the harbor, were twelve great Spanish ships loaded
with gold and silver. On the following day twelve
more arrived with the same sort of cargo. Hawkins
and Drake said to the Spaniards, "We wish to refit
our vessels and sail for home. If you will agree not to
interfere with us, we will not touch your ships." The
agreement was made, and for three days everything was
quiet and friendly. Then, in spite of all their promises,
the Spaniards suddenly made a fierce attack on the
English vessels. Hawkins in the Minion and Drake in
the Judith succeeded in escaping and making their
way to England; but the pearls and gold went to the
bottom of the Gulf of Mexico.

Drake reached home before the admiral, and told his
story of the treachery of the Spaniards. He had lost all
that he had invested, and he appealed to the queen to
oblige Spain to make his loss good. Queen Elizabeth
was not sure that England was strong enough to fight

with Spain, so she did nothing for him. Then Drake took matters into his own hands. He went on voyage after voyage. He robbed Spanish colonies, and he took Spanish gold and jewels wherever he could find them. King Philip of Spain complained bitterly of the "master thief of the western world," but the queen did not punish her seaman.

On one of his voyages Drake had landed on the Isthmus of Panama and made his way across it. When he reached the highest point of the isthmus, the Indians who were his guides showed him a tall tree. "Climb it," they said; and Drake obeyed eagerly. Steps had been cut into the tree, and soon he was on a little platform which was supported by the branches. Behold, a vast ocean was on either hand. "Behind you is the North Sea, from which you have come," said his guides, "and before you is the South Sea." "Into which I will go," said Drake to himself. "May God give me leave and life to sail an English ship on that sea but once!" he cried.

Year after year passed. One night a messenger came to Drake to say, "Her Majesty the Queen wishes to see you." The bluff sailor and the mighty sovereign had a long talk. Not many months later five ships sailed out of Plymouth Harbor under Drake's command. They were not only fully armed, but they were provided with all the luxuries of the time. The fragrance of costly perfumes floated back to the crowds on the wharf. The furnishings of the admiral's cabin were of the richest satin and velvet. The table was spread with the finest of linen and laid with dishes of silver and gold. When the commander was ready to dine, the sound of violins was heard, and the music continued until the meal was ended.

As the ship sailed away, some people on the wharf said, " I hope his voyage to Egypt will be a success." Others retorted, " Those ships will never see Egypt; they are going to trade and explore in the South Sea." Still others smiled knowingly and said to themselves, " The exploring will be searching for Spanish ships, and the trading will be seizing Spanish treasures." This last was exactly what Drake meant to do; but if a hint of his plans had reached Spain, the treasures would have been safely hidden. Sixty years earlier Magellan had sailed through the strait that bears his name, but no one else had ever succeeded in making the voyage. "What Magellan did, I can do," thought Drake, and he sailed down the coast of South America and steered boldly into the strait. Two vessels had already been broken up as unseaworthy; a fierce tempest scattered the other three; one sank; and the commander of the second went home in despair. For fifty-two days Drake was driven about by terrible storms. When the gales ceased, he found that his vessel was lying among a group of islands. He landed on the most southern and walked alone to its farthest extremity. There he stood looking at the breakers rolling up on the shore. Before him the waters of the Atlantic and the Pacific mingled. He threw himself on the ground, clasped his arms about a jagged rock, and said to himself, " I am the only man in the world who has ever been so far south."

The exciting part of the voyage was yet to come. Some of the treasure that the Spaniards took from Peru was carried to Panama by land, and some was loaded on shipboard and carried up the coast to the isthmus. One of these ships with a cargo of good yellow gold was lying in Valparaiso. The crew caught sight of white sails coming toward them. "See!" they cried. "There's one of our ships! Get the wine ready and we will make a night of it!" The flags were run up and the drums were beaten in welcome; but almost before the Spaniards had discovered their mistake, the Englishmen had seized the ship and fastened the men under the hatches. So it was that the Golden Hind went merrily up the coast, now and then seizing a vessel full of provisions or valuables. One day some of the men went ashore, and there they came across a man who had laid down his burden of silver bars and fallen asleep. "Pardon us, sir," they said with mock politeness in the best Spanish they could muster. "We are grieved to disturb you, but we will make amends. We will relieve

you of the weight of the silver, and then your journey
will be less wearisome."

Drake was aiming for Lima, where he expected to
find vessels worth capturing. The vessels were there,
but every ounce of treasure had either been taken ashore
or carried away two weeks earlier on a ship which was
known among sailors as the Spitfire. "We will catch
her," thought Drake, and he set out in pursuit. He
captured one ship. "Where is the Spitfire?" he demanded. "Ten days ahead," was the reply. The next
capture said, "Five days," and the next, "Two days."
Then Drake swung before the eyes of the sailors a
golden chain that gleamed and glittered in the sunshine.
"This goes to the man who sees the Spitfire first," he
said. A boy, Drake's own nephew, was the fortunate
one to win the reward. The Spitfire yielded without a
blow, and such a cargo went into the hold of the Golden
Hind as no English vessel had ever carried before:
thirteen chests of Spanish dollars, eighty pounds of
gold, twenty-six tons of silver, and more jewels than
could be counted. Two or three other vessels were
captured, but they proved to be loaded with silk and
linen and china, and there was little room for such
trifles in the treasure-laden hold. "I think her Majesty
will be satisfied with what I have done," said Drake to
himself, "and now we will make for home."

The Spaniards were keeping close watch of the strait;

but that did not trouble Drake in the least, for he had
another plan in his mind. Mariners believed that there
was a northern channel which led from the Pacific to
the Atlantic. The Northwest Passage they called it,
and Drake meant to find this passage and sail home
through it. Straight north went the gold-laden vessel.
The weather grew colder and colder, and when he was
as far north as Vancouver Island, he saw that it was of
no use to try to go farther. So he determined to reach
England by steering west across the Pacific and round-
ing the Cape of Good Hope. He went south again and
entered a harbor near where San Francisco now stands.
The cliffs were white like those of England. " In the
name of Queen Elizabeth," declared Drake, " I claim
this land for England, and I name it New Albion." He
set up a " fair great post," and to the post he fixed a
plate of metal marked with the date and the name of
the queen. So it was that the English paid their first
visit to the western shores of what is now the United
States.

Then the Golden Hind crossed the Pacific. Drake
fell among thievish savages, he ran upon a reef, and he
was caught in fearful gales; but at last he sailed into
Plymouth Sound, the first English captain who had
been around the world. His enemies were waiting for
" the pirate," as they called him, and King Philip was
clamoring for his punishment; but Queen Elizabeth

QUEEN ELIZABETH KNIGHTING DRAKE ON BOARD THE GOLDEN HIND
From a drawing by Sir John Gilbert

would not give up either Drake or the treasure that he
had brought. In a few months she went in all state to
dine with him on board his vessel. Before she left, she
made him a knight. Thousands of people visited the
Golden Hind, and she forbade that it should ever be
destroyed.

The queen was in need of brave sailors. A few years
later Philip prepared a great fleet to attack England.
He was so sure of victory that he called his fleet the
Invincible Armada. Sixty vessels had already assembled
off Lisbon and Cadiz. Here was a chance for Drake.
He set out with four of the queen's vessels and twenty-
six provided by merchants. Every one was eager to
have a share in the enterprise, for wherever Drake went
he found treasure. He sailed straight for Cadiz, and
before the Spaniards even guessed that their enemy was
at hand, he was burning ships and destroying stores.
This was all very well, but Drake did not mean to return to England empty-handed. He had heard that a
Portuguese vessel with a precious cargo was near the
Azores. He sailed out boldly, captured the ship, loaded
his vessel with a greater treasure than ever before, and
went home. He sent a gay little message to the queen
that he had "singed King Philip's beard." In reality
he had done so much harm to the Armada that it could
not sail for a whole year.

At last, however, the Armada came. The English

had made the best preparations that they could, and
their fleet lay off Plymouth. Drake and the other admirals were playing bowls on shore when suddenly a
man ran among them so out of breath that he could
only gasp, " The Spaniards, the Spaniards! They are
off the coast! " Two of the officers started for their
ships. But Drake called, " Gentlemen, let us go on with
our game: there will be time enough to beat the Spaniards afterwards." The game was played out, and then
the admirals went on board their vessels. The Spaniards
had a great many stately, top-heavy ships that they called
galleons; the English had a mongrel fleet made up of
almost all the kinds of craft that had ever been built.
If they had been willing to stand still and be fired at,
the Spaniards would probably have beaten; but a little
English boat, hardly longer than a fishing smack, would
dash up under the high guns of a galleon and fire a
shot or two. Then, before the clumsy Spanish vessel
could turn around, the English boat had slipped away
and was firing at another great war-ship. Drake was the
man of whom the Spaniards were most afraid. People
believed in magic in those days, and many a man whispered, " He has sold himself to the devil, and Satan is
helping him." They must almost have thought Drake
to be Satan himself when they knew his next exploit.
The English sent burning boats among the galleons.
In their fright the Spanish ships cut loose from their

anchors and soon were widely separated. Then was Drake's time. He dashed up to one after another and captured it, and with twelve of the great vessels in tow went back to the fleet. The winds and waves finished the work, and only sixty of Philip's ships ever went back to Spain.

Drake made another expedition across the Atlantic in quest of treasure, but it failed. The Spaniards had learned better how to meet "the dragon," as they called him, and they hid their riches more carefully. Sickness came upon the little company. Every day there were deaths. At last Drake himself fell ill and grew worse rapidly. The face of the surgeon was grave, and the men gathered in groups to talk of the suffering admiral.

" There will never be another man like him," they declared.

" No," said one, " he never forgot his men, and when there was a prize, he gave us the generous share."

" He was good to his prisoners, too," added another. " Any other man would have killed them, but he let them go free, and once he even gave them a vessel to go home in."

" He brought a stream of fresh water into Plymouth, and he and Sir John gave the Chatham Chest to help poor sailors."

" He never would let a church be burned or the house of any woman that begged for mercy."

So the men talked of their beloved commander. The fleet had anchored near the little island of Puerto Bello, and a few days later it sailed slowly out to sea, bearing the leaden coffin in which were the remains of the dead admiral. Trumpets were blown, cannon were fired, and then the body of the old hero was lowered solemnly and reverently into the ocean.

OUTLINE

The quest for gold in America — the boyhood of Francis Drake — he becomes a sailor — sells his boat — his voyage on the Judith — loss of the pearls and gold — his appeal to Queen Elizabeth for payment — his revenge on Spain — his first view of the South Sea — the queen sends for him — he sails on a mysterious voyage — the storm drives him "farthest south" — he seizes Spanish treasure on sea and on land — he pursues the Spitfire — the quest for the Northwest Passage — lands at "New Albion" — crosses the Pacific — the queen visits the Golden Hind — Philip plans to attack England — "singeing King Philip's beard" — the coming of the Armada — the sea fight — Drake's last voyage — his reputation among his men — his burial.

SUGGESTIONS FOR WRITTEN WORK

A day with Francis Drake in his boyhood.

Drake tells Queen Elizabeth of the behavior of the Spaniards at Vera Cruz.

Philip's appeal to Queen Elizabeth to punish Drake.

Drake tells his adventures to his nephew.

JOHN SMITH

THE FATHER OF VIRGINIA

DURING the century following Columbus's first voyage, the Spanish established colonies in the New World, but neither the French nor the English succeeded in making a permanent settlement. A few years after the death of Drake, a company of Englishmen determined to settle in America. One cold December morning their three little vessels sailed down the Thames River. "Good-by," shouted the people on the wharf. "Be sure to find the Northwest Passage!" cried one. "Make the Indians tell you what became of Raleigh's colony!" bade another; and a third called, "Don't forget to send us some pearls and a great lump of gold!"

The colonists were eager to be off, but they might as well have stayed at home a while longer, for the wind was contrary, and for six long weeks they could not get out of sight of England. At last, however, they were fairly at sea. They were crowded in the three small vessels, the voyage was long and wearisome, and they had nothing to do. They talked a great deal about a certain little box that was on board. King James liked to do the simplest things with a great air of mystery. So he had told them that the names of those who were to govern the colony were in the box, but he had forbidden it to be opened until they had reached Virginia. They talked, too, a great deal about one another. Some of the idle voyagers had the absurd notion that one man on board meant to murder the principal ones among them, and make himself king, and for thirteen weeks they kept him a close prisoner.

JOHN SMITH
From Smith's map of Virginia published in 1624

This man's name was John Smith. He was only twenty-eight years old, but he had had many strange experiences. His parents died when he was a boy. No one seemed to take any care of him, and he wandered away to France. He became a soldier, rose to be captain, was taken prisoner by the Turks, and made to wear a heavy iron ring about his neck. He escaped and found his way again to England, arriving in time to go to America with the colonists.

The ship came to what is now Virginia at the end of April, 1607, and after many weeks on the ocean, the

country seemed to the weary colonists a perfect fairyland. The air was soft and warm. There were tall trees,
green hills, rivers, and meadows. There were straw-
berries four times as large as those in England. There
were delicious oysters; and to make it seem even more
like fairyland, in some of the oysters there were beautiful pearls.

Glad as they were of both pearls and oysters, they
did not forget to open the little box. In it they found
that John Smith was named as one of the seven gov-
ernors; and it is hard to see how Jamestown, as the little
settlement had been named, could have lived without
him. Most of the colonists called themselves " gentlemen; " and according to their ideas, gentlemen were
men who never did any work, — the very worst kind of
people to come to a new country. The voyage had been
much longer than was expected, and there was little
left to eat but stale wheat and barley, and not much of
that. These helpless " gentlemen " quarreled like bad-
tempered children. One declared indignantly, " The
president would not give me a penny knife that I
wanted." " And he would not give my son a spoonful
of beer," added another. " I believe that he takes the
best of everything for himself," said a third. There was
one excuse for their quarreling, and that was that they
were all suffering. When a place was chosen for their
colony, no one had stopped to think whether it was

healthful or not, and they had settled on a little peninsula extending into the James River, because it could be easily protected against the Indians, and because the water was so deep that ships could be tied to the trees. When the hot sun began to beat down, however, the colonists sickened, and nearly two thirds of the whole number died.

Governor Smith made journeys up the rivers with chisels and hatchets and copper to exchange for corn; and whether the Indians wanted to trade or not, he always returned with a boatful of food. On one of these journeys he was captured by the savages; but instead of appearing frightened, he began to amuse the chief by showing him a pocket compass. A young brave was ill, and Smith said, " If you will let me send a leaf from my notebook to my friends, I will tell you where you will find a bottle of medicine for him." The bottle was found at the place that he named, and the savages began to be a little afraid of the man who could make a bit of paper talk. " Be one of our tribe," they said, " and show us how to attack the fort of the white men. You shall have some of our squaws for wives." Smith did not agree to this, so they carried him to their King Powhatan. A grave council was held, and it was decided that the prisoner should be put to death. He was tied fast and laid upon the ground. The Indians stood over him with heavy clubs ready to strike; but suddenly the king's little daughter Pocahontas threw her arms about him. Among the Indians, if a woman had lost a relative in battle, she was free to adopt a prisoner in his place if she chose, and the Indians must have been amused to see the little

POCAHONTAS

After the original painting now in possession of the Rolfe family

girl playing the part of a grown woman. Then, too, there was that compass, and if they killed a man who owned so wonderful a thing, there was no knowing what might happen to them. Powhatan turned away, saying, " Let him live. He shall make hatchets for me and copper bells and beads for my daughter." After Smith had been with them about a month, Powhatan said, " You are one of us now, and you may go back to your white friends if you choose."

Smith went back, and the time of his coming was a happy one in Jamestown, for on that day a ship sailed

in from England bringing new colonists. Unfortunately, however, most of them were like the other " gentlemen." They had no thought of going to work, but
began to search for gold. They found plenty of glittering bits of mica, and they discovered some yellow stones
all bright and shining. " Hurrah for the gold ! " they
cried, and they sent a whole shipload of the worthless
stuff back to England.

Now the company of merchants and others who had
paid the expenses of carrying the colonists across the
ocean began to feel as if they ought to have some return for their money. America was full of treasures,
they believed, and they wrote, " Why do you not send
us a lump of gold to show that you are really doing
something ? You seem to stay around Jamestown all
the time; why don't you explore the country and find
a passage to China ? " The company sent a command
which they probably thought sure to win the friendship
of the Indians. " Go to King Powhatan," they said,
" and crown him Emperor of Virginia." Half a dozen
blue beads or a new hatchet would have pleased Powhatan more than a coronet; but the company must be
obeyed, so he was crowned. He was a little afraid of
the long scarlet cloak that they wanted to lay upon his
shoulders. " It won't hurt you," whispered one of his
braves who had been to England with the whites; and
the " Emperor of Virginia " allowed it to be thrown

around him. The volley fired in his honor gave him a
terrible fright, but at last the absurd performance was
over. The "Emperor" graciously presented the whites
with his old blanket to send to King James, and the
colonists went back to Jamestown.

All this nonsense must have disgusted Captain Smith.
He said nothing, however, but set to work to get together as much tar, pitch, potash, and clapboards as he
could to send to England. He also sent a letter to the
company which must have made them open their eyes.
He told them how foolish it was to expect colonists to
find gold mines or even to send home great cargoes of
tar, when they had all they could do to defend themselves and get something to eat. "You sent us a ship,"
he said, " but the captain stayed here so long that, little
corn as there was, we had to give him three hogsheads
for the voyage home. Most of the men that you send us
are of no use. Give us thirty carpenters, gardeners,
blacksmiths, men who can work, rather than a thousand
of such as we have."

There were other troubles than the laziness of the
men, for the "Emperor of Virginia" was not pleased
when he found that they meant to stay, and he made
a plan to destroy the whole colony. He would probably
have succeeded if the child Pocahontas had not been so
friendly to the white men. One dark night she slipped
away from her home and ran through the woods to

Jamestown. "My father means to attack you," she whispered, and then she hurried away. Powhatan must have been amazed when a few days later Smith sent him a message, "We are all ready for you. Come whenever you choose."

So it was that John Smith watched over the colony. He got food from the Indians when no one else could succeed. He made the company understand that even in America lumps of gold were not lying about on the banks of every river. Perhaps his greatest achievement was making the lazy colonists work. They all expected to be served with rations whether they helped dig and plant, make clapboards, and build houses, or wandered about searching for pearls. When Smith became president of the colony, he declared, "No one will receive any rations who does not labor six hours a day." So the idle people had to take up their axes and hoes and go to work.

After two years of these struggles, while Smith lay asleep in his boat one day, a bag of gunpowder exploded and injured him so severely that his only hope of life was to go to England for treatment. For several years there were no more voyages of discovery for him, but during that time he wrote an interesting book about his life in Virginia. He never saw Jamestown again, but news of the little settlement came to him over the sea. The colonists were in sore need of his good sense, for they were in constant trouble. More and more men had gone to Virginia till there were in all nearly five hundred. Then came a terrible winter when food could not be had, — a winter that was always spoken of as the " Starving Time." In the spring only sixty colonists were left alive, and there would have been even fewer if Pocahontas had not often contrived to send them corn and meat. No help came from England, and at last the little company of suffering people set out in their small boats, hoping to get to Newfoundland and to find there some vessel that would carry them home. They did not dream that English vessels loaded with provisions were just off the mouth of the river. Soon, however, they discovered them. So they went back to Jamestown, and the colony was saved. A gentleman named John Rolfe began to raise tobacco. His neighbors did the same; and after that there was no fear of starving, for Virginia tobacco always brought a good price.

These were some of the bits of news that came to Captain Smith from the colony that he had saved and guarded; but one day he heard something that must have brought his life in America even more vividly before him — the Lady Rebekah was on her way to England. This Lady Rebekah was the little Pocahontas, now grown to a tall young woman and married to John Rolfe. She was presented at court and entertained

THE MARRIAGE OF POCAHONTAS

by the Bishop of London; but she was not at all taken aback by the city or the great folk whom she met. "She carries herself as the daughter of a king," declared a writer of the time. Of course Captain Smith went to see her. He saluted her most respectfully, but she was not pleased at his deference. "When you were in Powhatan's land, you called him father," she said; "and now that I am in your land, you must call me your child and let me call you father."

Captain Smith had no idea of giving up the business of exploring, and after a while he made several trips to what is now New England. He drew maps of the coast, he caught fish, he searched for gold mines, he bought furs of the Indians, and he tried hard to found a colony. The last years of his life were spent in writing. He wrote five or six books about America, an interesting account of his adventures, and "A Sea Grammar," to teach how a ship should be built, rigged, and managed.

Off the coast of New Hampshire is a little group of tiny islands, the Isles of Shoals, hardly more than barren rocks. Here it is probable that Smith landed, and on one of them a monument was long ago placed in his memory. It could hardly have been reared in honor of a man who was a braver explorer, a more unselfish colonizer, or a better friend to any American colony in its early days of suffering and struggle.

OUTLINE

English colonists start for America — the long voyage — idle talk on board — John Smith's early life — landing in Virginia — opening the mysterious box — the quarrelsome "gentlemen" — sickness at Jamestown — Governor Smith captured by the Indians — Pocahontas defends him — arrival of new colonists — their "gold" — the demands of the company — crowning Powhatan — Governor Smith's letter to the company — the kindness of Pocahontas — Smith's treatment of the lazy colonists — he leaves Virginia — the Starving Time — how the colony was saved — tobacco raising — Pocahontas in England — Smith's last years — his monument.

SUGGESTIONS FOR WRITTEN WORK

The colonists' first day in Virginia.

Powhatan describes his coronation.

A colonist writes a letter home beginning, "We had a very hard winter." Finish the letter.

SAMUEL DE CHAMPLAIN

THE FOUNDER OF QUEBEC

WHILE Spain and England were interested in the New World, it was not forgotten by the French explorers and fur-traders. On one of the fur-trading expeditions a young man named Samuel de Champlain was sent by the French king to see as much of the country about the St. Lawrence as he could and write a journal about his expedition.

When he came home, he published his journal. The French began to say, "The Spanish have a 'New Spain' in America; why should we not have a 'New France'?" Before long three ships sailed away, not only to trade, but to make a settlement. Champlain was one of the leaders. They chose for their colony a little island at the mouth of the St. Croix River. "It is sure to be warm and pleasant here," they thought, "for it is no farther north than the southern part of our own France."

CHAMPLAIN
CHAMPLAIN

They set to work to build houses for themselves. They mounted their cannon and laid out little flower gardens. Champlain took great pains to water his flowers, but the sun was so hot that it scorched them. The mosquitoes bit savagely, and the men had to work with all their might; but they were happy, and when the ship returned to France, they bade her a cheerful farewell. They had no idea what was before them; but soon the wind grew bitterly cold, the water froze, the ground froze, even the cider froze and was served in chunks and splinters. Wood was scarce, for masses of ice barred the river and shut them from the forests of the mainland. Half of the company died. " Oh, if the ship would only come again!" they groaned. At last the ship came. "We will not stay here another winter," the colonists declared, and Champlain set out to find a better place for their settlement.

After a long search, he finally chose a place in Nova Scotia near where Annapolis now stands. Then there was a moving day indeed, for they moved not only their clothes and axes and kettles and cannon, but even the houses,—at least those that could be taken apart easily and put on board the ship. They were full of courage when they landed. "Look at that range of hills!" they cried. "No cold winds will blow through those. We will build tighter houses, too, and make sure of having wood enough."

Food was plenty, and good times were plenty, for fifteen of the principal men formed a society which they named " The Order of Mirth." They took turns in being Grand Master, and the one who held the office for the day must provide for the table. He might hunt or fish or buy of the Indians, but in some way he must secure a dinner. When dinner time came, the little procession marched into the dining room. The Grand Master led the way. A napkin was thrown over his shoulder, and an ornamented collar, the badge of the order, was around his neck. The other men followed, each one carrying his plate. The Indians sat about on the floor, waiting for their share of the feast, and gazing with grave amusement at the strange pranks of their white friends.

So the time passed and spring came. The colonists had a water-mill, and they were making and burning brick. Champlain had laid out his garden as usual, and they were ready for a busy and happy summer. They never dreamed that a ship was on the ocean with a letter that said they must come home, because the people who sent out the colony could not support it any longer.

Every one was filled with regret. "The hardest time was over," they said gloomily. "We had just found out how to live here." "I'll come back and make my home in this place," declared one, "if I have to come alone with my wife and the children."

Champlain was sadly disappointed at having to leave Nova Scotia, but he packed up his journal and the maps and sea charts that he had made and began to think what to do next. A place that he had seen on the St. Lawrence kept coming before his mind. "The river is narrow there," he said to himself. "That high hill could be easily fortified, and the little stream that flows down beside it on the north would help to defend it. The Indians are friendly and will listen to us when we tell them of the Christian faith. 'Kebec,' as they call it, is the very place for a fur station and for a colony."

He had no money to send out ships, so he appealed

for help to a wealthy nobleman in Paris. This nobleman read Champlain's journal, and pored over its maps
and pictures. At last he said, "I'll found a colony at
Kebec, provided you will be its governor." So in the
summer of 1608, one year after the settlement of Jamestown, a shipload of eager French colonists landed on
the flats in the shadow of the towering cliff of Kebec,
or Quebec, as they spelled it.

There was enough for every one to do, and they set to
work to clear the ground and build their houses. Champlain kept a journal of course, and in it he drew a picture of the cluster of build-
ings. It must have looked
quite like some old castle;
for there was a moat and
a drawbridge, platforms
for the cannon, a store-
house, a forge, and three
houses, each two stories
high. Nor did Champlain
forget his flower garden.

CHAMPLAIN'S DRAWING OF QUEBEC
IN 1613

He liked birds as well as
flowers, and he had a dovecote that looks in the picture
half as large as one of the houses.

The winter was long and cold. Sickness came upon
the colonists and many died. It was an even harder
winter for the Indians, and they often came to the

fort to beg the kind-hearted governor for food. These Indians were Algonquins, and to the south of them, in what is now New York, were the Iroquois, their bitter enemies. "We shall go on the warpath after the winter is over," the Algonquins told Champlain, and they looked longingly at the "fire-sticks" of the Frenchmen. Then said Champlain, "I want to see the country to the southward. If you will guide me, I will help you against the Iroquois." The Algonquins were overjoyed. "The great governor is going to kill the Iroquois with his fire-sticks," they said.

When spring came, a party of Indians, together with Champlain and two other Frenchmen, paddled up the St. Lawrence and the Richelieu rivers and down the lake which was afterwards named for Champlain. Every day brought them nearer the Iroquois, and at last they saw the canoes of their enemies. "Go home and plant corn!" shouted the Iroquois. "You can't fight!"

"We'll go home and take you with us!" retorted the Algonquins.

Both parties made ready for battle. In the morning the Algonquins dashed forward. Then came the great surprise of the day, for Champlain fired his gun. Two of the Iroquois fell. The others stood for a moment motionless. A second Frenchman fired, and the Iroquois ran as if the witches were after them. This little fight in the wilderness was really an important action, for from that day the fierce Iroquois were bitter enemies of the French.

Champlain made several journeys to France. On one of these he was married to a child of twelve. Little Hélène was left there in school for a few years, while her explorer husband went back to his colony over the seas. He did not forget his child wife, however, and he gave her name to an island in the river.

On Champlain's first voyage to the St. Lawrence, the Indians had told him of a salt sea to the northward. He longed to go in search of it, and now he had good reason to think that he could find it. A young man who had spent the winter among the Indians returned to Paris and declared that he had been up the Ottawa River, and near its head had found a sea of salt water. Every one was interested, for this was thought to be surely the Northwest Passage. Champlain and the young man went back to Quebec and set out to find the way to India. They went up the Ottawa River to Allumette Island, and Champlain said to the Indians, " This young man says he went north last winter to the great salt sea. Will you give me guides so I can go to it ? "

The chief looked sternly at the young man and demanded, " Did you go to the great salt sea last winter ? "

" Yes," he replied falteringly.

The chief turned his back upon him. " The fellow is a great liar," he said to Champlain. " He was with us all winter. He slept in that wigwam every night. Give him to us and we will see to it that he does not tell any more lies."

Then the young man confessed that he had made up the whole story to win attention in Paris, and that he had not dreamed of Champlain's trying to make the journey. "If you will only pardon me," he pleaded, "I will go north next summer till I find whether there is a sea or not." And Champlain, disappointed as he was, pardoned him.

So the life of the governor of Quebec went on. He explored; he helped the Algonquins in their raids against the Iroquois, spending one whole winter among them; he established a fur station at Montreal; and he carried out a plan that was very dear to him of bringing over from France four missionaries to tell the Indians of the Christian faith. They had a good helper in the wife of Champlain. In the years when her explorer husband was going back and forth between France and America, the little Hélène had grown up, and when she was twenty-two she came to Quebec. "A brave girl," her brother called her when he met her at the wharf. She was much interested in the shy little Indian children, and set to work at once to learn their language so as to talk with them and teach them. They were soon her devoted friends, and the braves and squaws almost worshiped her.

There were many hard years for the colony on the
rock, but at last a summer came when all things promised well. Champlain was making ready to welcome
the ships from France with supplies for the winter; but

France and England
were at war, and sud-
denly six English ves-
sels appeared off Que-
bec. The commander
sent a polite note to the
governor, demanding
the surrender of the
place. Champlain in his
reply signed himself
"Your affectionate ser-
vant," just as the Eng-
lish commander had
done, but he boldly re-
fused to surrender. The
Englishman did not

THE TAKING OF QUEBEC
From an engraving of 1698

know that the company had not kept the fortifications
in repair, and that food was so scanty that the men were
allowed only seven ounces of dried peas a day. He
sailed away from Quebec, but he captured the supply
ships at the mouth of the river, so no food came to the
colony all that long winter. They divided the peas by
count; they bought all the moose meat that the Indians

would spare; they fished as much as their few lines and hooks would permit; and they ate every kind of root that was fit for food.

When even the roots seemed to be giving out, English war-ships appeared again and demanded surrender; and Champlain, brave old soldier as he was, was forced to give up without firing a gun. He had to leave Quebec; but when the treaty between the two countries was signed, Canada was given back to France, and he was again made governor. One morning in May, the people in Quebec were aroused at sunrise by the firing of cannon. They were in a great fright; but it did not last long, for soon their beloved governor stepped ashore. Up the hill to the fortress he went, escorted by a company of French soldiers. Flags waved, drums beat, and cheer followed cheer, for Champlain had come again to the people who loved him so well. Far back into the forests the word went swiftly from one tribe of red men to another that the governor had come, and hundreds of them hastened to Quebec to welcome him. For three years longer he worked and planned for the land that he loved; and when the end came, he died in the fort on the rock, a brave explorer, a wise governor, a true friend and helper of every one around him.

OUTLINE

Champlain and his journal of the St. Lawrence voyage — the French colony at the St. Croix — moving to Nova Scotia — "the Order of Mirth" — the colonists return to France — Champlain plans a colony at Quebec — the new settlement on the St. Lawrence — the first winter in Quebec — Champlain's agreement with the Algonquins — the expedition against the Iroquois — Champlain's marriage — his search for the Northwest Passage — mission work — the coming of the English vessels — hard times in Quebec — the surrender of the colony — Champlain's return to Quebec.

SUGGESTIONS FOR WRITTEN WORK

A letter from the St. Croix settlement.
"Hélène" tells what she saw when she reached Quebec.
Champlain describes his return to Quebec.

MILES STANDISH

COMMANDER-IN-CHIEF OF THE PILGRIMS

ONE cold winter day, thirteen years after the founding of Jamestown, a ship was tossing about in the wild breakers off the coast of Cape Cod. It had been on the ocean for more than two months, much of the time in gales and tempests. Once the sailors had rebelled and declared that it must return to England. "We won't risk our lives in the shattered old hulk," they said; but the leaky seams were calked as best they could be

and the vessel sailed on. The passengers had expected
to go farther south, but the storms had driven them far
out of their course, and they saw that the best thing to
do was to get inside the point of Cape Cod for shelter.

THE DEPARTURE OF THE PILGRIMS
From a painting by C. W. Cope

These people had not come to America to find lumps
of gold or to search for the Northwest Passage; they
had come, men, women, and children, to make themselves homes in the New World. In England, as in
most other places at that time except Holland, people
were obliged by law to attend the same church as the

king; and if they did not, they were fined or imprisoned or sometimes put to death. And yet, when they wanted to leave the kingdom, King James forbade their going! A little company, however, succeeded in escaping to Holland. They lived there for twelve years; but they were English, and badly as their country had treated them, they loved it. They could not bear to have their children speak Dutch and grow up Dutch rather than English. So they concluded to go to America, where they could worship God as they thought would be pleasing to Him and bring up their boys and girls to be English men and women. King James would not give them a charter, a parchment saying that they had a right to settle in America; but he said rather grudgingly that they might go if they wished, and so long as they " carried themselves peaceably," he would not molest them.

Only a very hard-hearted ruler would have troubled these honest, earnest people, for they certainly had enough to bear. They had come in the middle of the winter to a wild country, full of unknown dangers. It was bitterly cold. Icy rain and snow and sleet fell upon them as if trying to drive them from the land. Food was none too plenty, and the captain was saying, " Whatever happens, I shall keep enough for my crew on the way back." The sailors muttered, " If they don't get a place soon, we 'll drop them and their goods on the shore and leave them."

There was nothing to do but to search for a place at once, and a company of explorers set out. The one and only soldier among them was made the leader. His name was Miles Standish. They were put ashore near the end of Cape Cod; and, waving a farewell to their friends on board the Mayflower, started off boldly on their exploring trip. After going a mile or two, they saw five or six Indians and a dog. They were glad, for they hoped to make friends with them; but the Indians whistled to the dog and ran into the woods. The next interesting sight was some heaps of earth that had evidently just been piled up, for they could see the marks of fingers where the Indians had patted and smoothed the sides. Within these mounds were big baskets of corn. They had never seen Indian corn before, but they knew it must be some kind of grain and good to eat. "Shall we take it?" they questioned. Finally they decided to carry it home, and, when they met the Indians, to pay them well for it. They saw rivers and ponds and deer and geese. They saw, too, a trap that had been set for deer; and before he knew it, one of the gallant explorers was caught by the leg and tossed up into the air.

Again and again the colonists searched for a good place to make their home; but when they returned to the Mayflower and their friends called, "Have you found it yet?" they could only say, "Not yet." At

THE PILGRIMS ON THE MAYFLOWER
From the painting by Henry Oliver Walker in the State House at Boston

last there came a day when they replied, " We have found a place where the soil seems better than any we have seen before. It is marked 'Plymouth' on John Smith's map. There is clay for bricks, good sand for mortar, and stone for wells and chimneys."

" Is there any river ? "

" Not large enough for boats, but there are several streams of good clear water."

" Did you see any Indians ? "

" No, but we saw clearings that looked as if they had planted corn there three or four years ago. The land rises from the water to a high hill. We climbed to the top, and we could see a long way over the country. That hill would be just the place to mount our cannon. There is a spring of good water on the hillside, and we can put our houses near it."

There was no question that this was the best site they had found, and very soon a boat left the Mayflower, landed its passengers on a great rock at the water's edge, and went back for another load. There were no idlers at Plymouth; as soon as a man was set ashore, he went to work. The first thing to do was to build a log house large enough to hold their goods and to shelter the women and children from the rain—and those first weeks it seemed to rain most of the time. The women, too, were hard at work, cooking at camp-fires; and even the little children ran about and gathered twigs for the fires.

The Pilgrims, as they were called from their wanderings, had heard frightful stories of the fierceness of the Indians, but there were other troubles than fear of savages. Food was scanty and sickness came upon them. They had been in Plymouth only a month when Rose Standish, wife of the captain, died. He himself was well; and he went about from one bed to another, doing everything that he could to help the sick and suffering. At last the spring came, but half of the whole number were dead. The Indians did not molest the white men, but it was plain that they were watching closely. " How many camp-fires did you see last night ? " the settlers would ask those whose turn it had been to keep guard. The number grew larger night by night. The men worked as fast as they could to get their log huts done, so they could have some little protection, for they were afraid that the savages meant to unite and come in large numbers to attack them. They did not dare to raise mounds over the graves of those that died lest the Indians should count them and see how few were left. Sometimes in the darkness they could hear the yells of the savages. One day Miles Standish and another man left their axes in the woods while they went home to dinner; and when they returned, they found that the Indians had stolen them.

The colonists met to decide who should be their leader if the Indians should make an attack. There was not much question about it with one brave, well-trained soldier among them. Of course they chose Miles Standish, and they all agreed to obey his orders. While they were talking, one of the men said softly, " Look — over on that hill! " There stood two Indians beckoning, and Captain Standish and one other man went out boldly, hoping to make friends with them. They carried only one musket, and soon they laid that down to show that they were not enemies; but the two red men ran away. As the colonists stood and listened, they could hear the sound of many Indians running through the woods, but not one was to be seen. " The cannon must be mounted at once," declared the captain. So the three cannon were dragged to the top of the hill.

The next Indian they saw, however, was not in the least afraid of them or their cannon. He walked boldly along close to the little houses; and when the men stood before him with their guns, he did not turn back, but said cordially, " Welcome, Englishmen, welcome! " He told them that his name was Samoset, that he had been near Monhegan Island and had learned a little English from the fishermen who went there. He was ready to tell all that he knew, and he knew many things that the colonists wanted to hear. He said that some of the Indians were angry with the English because an English captain had captured twenty-seven of their tribe and carried them away to Spain to sell as slaves. He talked all the afternoon except when he was eating, — no small part of the time. At dusk the English tried to say farewell to him, but he said he was willing to stay all night. So they made him a bed; but they kept watch of him, for no one knew but he might be a spy. In the morning he said, " Good-by; I am going to visit Massasoit, the chief of the Wampanoags." And he went away happy with a knife, a bracelet, and a ring.

It was not long before Samoset came again; and this time he brought a friend, Squanto, one of the very men who had been carried off by the English captain. A kind-hearted Englishman had rescued him and sent him home. Squanto could talk English very well. After a little while he said, "Massasoit, chief of the Wampanoags, and sixty braves are coming to see you." And even while they were talking, Massasoit and his warriors came marching across the crest of a hill to the south of the settlement. " They cannot come into the village," declared Captain Standish. Squanto went back and forth with messages, and it was decided that Massasoit and twenty braves, unarmed, might enter. To show the chieftain due honor, a drum was beaten, a trumpet was blown, and six muskets were fired. After a long talk, Massasoit and the whites agreed to be friends and to help each other in war if there should be need.

It seemed as if need would soon come, for one day a

strange Indian strode into the little village, bringing
a bundle of arrows wrapped in a rattlesnake's skin.
Squanto explained that Canonicus, King of the Narragansetts, was angry because they had made friends with
his enemy Massasoit and that the arrows meant war.
" If he will have war, let him! " cried the captain; and
he stuffed the snakeskin with bullets and powder. " Tell
Canonicus," the settlers bade their messenger, " that we
do not wish to fight, but if he does, we are ready for
him." Canonicus was a badly frightened Indian when he
saw the snakeskin. It seemed that Squanto had wished
to give the impression that his English friends were all-
powerful, and he had declared that they kept the plague
in a box to let it loose when they chose. The chief was
afraid it had come.

But Canonicus's fright might not last long, so the
captain decided that it was best to make the village
stronger. They built a close high fence, or palisade, of
stout posts around the group of houses, and the captain reviewed his little army of forty-eight men and
appointed an officer for every twelve. They built a
strong fort with a heavy flat roof on the top of the hill.
This building was church as well as fort. When Sunday morning came, the drum was beaten, and the men
assembled before the captain's door, muskets in hand.
They took their places three abreast. The last in the
line was the governor, tall and dignified in his long

black robe. On his right hand the minister walked, and on his left strode Captain Standish. Behind them came the women and children. In this order they marched into the fort and seated themselves, each man with his musket beside him. Over their heads, on the

PILGRIMS GOING TO CHURCH
From a painting by G. H. Boughton

thick flat roof, the cannon were mounted; and so they were ready either to listen to the sermon or to fight the Indians if an attack was made.

The colonists had to be on their guard all the time; but although there had been many alarms, there had been no fighting since they had landed at Plymouth. The Indians knew that their only hope of getting the better of the whites was by surprising them, and they never could surprise the captain, for he was always ready for an attack. He showed them that he wished to be friendly, but that he would not be imposed upon; and once when a sachem, or under-chief, had seized Squanto, he had set out in the night with but ten men, dashed into the large wigwam, and demanded either his friend Squanto or the sachem who had murdered him. The story of his courage went from one tribe to another, and many sachems sent messengers to ask for the friendship of the whites.

The Pilgrims were so fair and just to the Indians that they would perhaps have had little trouble with them, had it not been for some new companies of colonists that came from England and settled near them. Many of these newcomers were dishonest. They cheated and abused the Indians shamefully. "We will kill them all," said the red men.

"But the little captain at Plymouth," objected one, "he and his men will avenge them."

"We will kill him and his friends at Plymouth, too," declared the plotters.

The Pilgrims heard of this, and they said, "We must fight." Then Captain Standish and eight men set out for the new settlement. Soon four Indians came boldly up to the house where he and four other Englishmen were waiting. "We are not afraid of your little captain," cried the red men. "He thinks he can kill us, but let him try." They pushed into the house, and the other Indians crowded around it. ".Go and live with the women, little captain," they called, "you are no fighter!" One of them began to whet his knife. "My knife eats, it does not speak," he said. Then the "little captain," as strong and wiry as he was slender, sprang upon the tall savage, caught his knife away from him, and killed him with his own weapon. Two of the others were also killed, and one carried away as prisoner. This was the first time that an Indian had been slain by the Pilgrims. It was the custom in England then to put the heads of criminals on posts in some public place to serve as a warning to all who passed by; so the head of the Indian leader was put up on the fort.

As the years passed, many other colonists came to Plymouth. More land was needed, and some of the settlers moved to places near by where they found fertile ground. Captain Standish and the minister, Elder Brewster, made homes for themselves nine miles to the north of Plymouth. The home of the captain's ancestors in England was called Duxbury, and this name was given to his new abode across the bay. There the two friends cut down the trees, and cleared fields for plowing. Whenever there was any trouble, however, the Pilgrims always sent for the captain, and he was ready for whatever must be done.

Once he had to leave his peaceful home to fight with the Pequots of Connecticut. These Pequots, the fiercest warriors of the wilderness, were determined to destroy the whites. They began by hanging around the settle- ments, and often when a few men went out to work in the woods or the fields, these savages would seize them and put them to death with most fearful tortures. The colonies decided to unite and strike one blow that should end such deeds. Plymouth sent fifty soldiers, and of course Captain Standish was called upon to lead them. The Pequots had built a strong palisade around their houses; but the English came upon them in the dark, got possession of the two entrances, and set fire to the fort. Nearly all the Pequots perished. It was a dread- ful scene, but it freed the settlers from all trouble with the Indians for forty years.

The last days of Miles Standish passed quietly and happily. It was not at all lonely at his house on "Cap- tain's Hill," for he had married a second time, and he had four sons and a daughter. Besides Elder Brewster, John Alden and others of his friends made their homes near him. Among them was his faithful Indian friend, Hob- bomak, who built himself a wigwam near the house of his captain. When he grew old and feeble, the stern fighter of the red men took the red man to his own house, and cared for him tenderly to the end of his life.

OUTLINE

The hard voyage of the colonists — why they had come to America — their troubles on reaching land — searching for a home — Plymouth — landing at Plymouth — hunger and sickness — fear of the Indians — choosing a captain — going to meet the Indians — the coming of Samoset — what he told the white men — Squanto — the visit of Massasoit — the message of Canonicus — the settlers' reply — Canonicus's fright — the settlers prepare for war — going to church — why the settlers were not attacked — the rescue of Squanto — the new colonists make trouble — the "little captain" fights with the Indians — the founding of Duxbury — the war with the Pequots — the last days of Miles Standish.

SUGGESTIONS FOR WRITTEN WORK

A Puritan boy writes home of his first day at Plymouth.

Samoset describes his first visit to Plymouth.

Two pilgrims talk together in Holland about going to America: one wishes to go, the other does not.

PETER STUYVESANT

LAST DUTCH GOVERNOR OF NEW YORK

WHILE England was sending colonists to Virginia, and France was making a settlement on the St. Lawrence, another European country was planning not to be shut out of the New World. This was Holland. One of her ships under Henry Hudson ex-

plored the Hudson River, and soon the Dutch founded
trading posts along its banks, and extended them almost
as far south as where Philadelphia now stands. All this
country between the Hudson and the Delaware they
called New Netherland. Their most flourishing settlement was on Manhattan Island. This was named New
Amsterdam. One morning in May, 1647, there was great
excitement in the little Dutch village. All the people
put on their Sunday clothes and went down to the bank
of the East River. "He's coming!" cried some one,
and they were so glad that they all shouted their welcome, though the vessel was much too far away for
the new governor to hear them. It came slowly up the
East River and anchored off the fort. Then the cannon
blazed out a greeting; the people shouted louder than
ever; the governor was rowed ashore and marched up
the street to the fort in all the glories of gold lace
and ruffles, drum and fife, and an escort of soldiers.
"He came like a peacock, with great state and pomp,"
wrote some one of his arrival.

This governor, Peter Stuyvesant, made a speech to
the people. "I shall rule you as a father rules his children," he said. They all cheered, for they did not know
that he meant that he should do exactly as he chose
and that they must obey him. He began by making laws
and seeing to it that they were enforced. He forbade
selling liquor to the Indians. Whoever broke this law

had to pay for all the damage that the drunken Indian might do. It was forbidden to build any more wooden chimneys. When a house was burned, four fire-wardens were to look into the matter. If they decided that the owner had been care-less, he had to pay a fine besides losing his house. This fine went to help buy hooks and ladders and leather fire-buckets for future emergencies.

The colony grew fast, and after a while it began to call itself a city. It was a very quiet, village-like lit-tle city, even though it was giving up its wooden buildings and thatched roofs. Every citizen who could af-

PETER STUYVESANT

ford it made the end of his house which fronted the street of little yellow and black bricks brought from Holland and arranged in checker-board fashion. The roofs were gorgeous with yellow and black tiles. These Dutchmen liked plenty of room for themselves and their

homes, and every one wanted to have around his house
a garden where he could raise vegetables and flowers
and plant the tulip bulbs that came from Holland. He
wanted a horse, a cow, some hens, and a pig or two.
Every morning the town herdsman drove the cows to
pasture; and every night he drove them back, leaving
each cow at her own gate, and blowing a horn to let
her master know she had come.

Within the house, there was one room that was kept
sacred from common use. This was the parlor, and
there the household treasures were collected. Car-
pets had not yet come into use, but fine sand was first
sprinkled upon the floor and then a broom was drawn
over it lightly in graceful figures. There was a high-
posted bedstead in the parlor, heaped up with a thick
feather bed, which only the skillful housewife knew how
to make round and smooth. There was a down quilt,
and there were heavy curtains and a valance. Two other
pieces of furniture were the special pride of the good
housekeeper. One was a solid oaken chest. When the
lid was raised there was a gleam of snowy linen, spun
and woven by the busy hands of the women of the household, and bleached on the grass to a dazzling whiteness.
The second was a cupboard, always made with glass
doors, for its duty was not to hide the silver and por-
celain but to show it. There were no rocking chairs
or sofas in the Dutch parlor, or anywhere else in the

house for that matter; and how the good people could
ever have felt comfortable, as they sat up straight

NEW AMSTERDAM IN STUYVESANT'S TIME

and stiff in the leather-covered, high-backed chairs, is a
mystery.

The parlor was used on festive occasions only; the
kitchen was the home room. There was the immense
fireplace with pothooks and crane. There were dressers
with rows of pewter plates and mugs and porringers
that must never be allowed to become dull if their mistress hoped to be called a good housekeeper. There was
a heavy square dining table, wide and roomy, for the
Dutch wives and daughters knew well how to cook deli-

cious dishes, and the husbands and sons knew how to
appreciate them.

Those early New Yorkers were sociable people, and
they did not by any means give all their time to spinning
and cooking and planting gardens. There were quilt-
ings and huskings and apple-paring bees; there were
birthday parties and weddings; there were parties at
New Year and Easter and Christmas and between times.
When one was to take place, the gentlemen made themselves gorgeous in their coats of silk or plush or velvet,
trimmed with lace and big, round silver buttons. These
coats came down almost to their ankles. Their shoes
were fastened with broad silver buckles. The ladies wore
jackets, and skirts which were almost as short as the
men's coats were long. These skirts were quilted in
patterns until they were fairly stiff with the stitching.
Below the skirt were home-knit stockings of red or blue
or green, and high-heeled shoes. Rings and brooches
were much worn; but the one ornament that every Dutch
lady felt she really could not do without was gold beads,
strings upon strings of them, to wind about her neck.

The great merrymaking of the year was at Christmas.
The Pilgrims had seen that holiday made the excuse for
so much drinking and low amusement in England that
they were determined to have no Christmas celebrations;
but the Dutch saw no reason why both grown-ups and
children should not enjoy the day, or rather, days, for

one was not nearly enough for the general jollity
and merriment. No one did any more work than was
really necessary during that time. The night before

A DUTCH HOUSE ON SANTA CLAUS MORNING

Christmas the children all hung up their stockings in
the chimney corner. Then they joined hands and sang
a song to Santa Claus which ended,

> " If you 'll to me a present give,
> I 'll serve you truly while I live."

As the years passed, there was more silver plate in the houses and handsomer furniture was brought from Holland. There were velvet chairs, watches, clocks, silken gowns, jewelry, broadcloth suits, embroidered purses, shirts and neckcloths trimmed with lace, and breeches made of silk and flowered with silver and gold. More colonists had come, and New Amsterdam was quite a different place in 1664 from what it had been in 1647 when the whole village turned out to welcome the new governor. For seventeen years he had ruled the Dutch town, and he had done well by it, for he was honest and he meant to do what he thought was for the best. He had treated the Indians kindly but firmly, and there had been little trouble with them. Difficulties were soon to appear, however. One day a young man who had just come from Boston to New Amsterdam told the governor some startling news. "King Charles of England has given this land to his brother James, the Duke of York," he said, "and there is a rumor that a fleet of armed vessels is already on the way to take possession of it."

Then there was excitement from one end of the Dutch city to the other. The governor bought powder and food and did his best to strengthen his fortifications. He had but one hundred soldiers, one little fort, a few guns and a small supply of powder. The three-foot wall of earth and the crumbling wooden palisade might help to keep out the arrows of the Indians, but they would be small protection against King Charles's cannon balls. Still the governor had no thought of surrender. He "stumped" about from one place to another, giving orders to the men who were working on the fortifications, sometimes encouraging them, sometimes storming at them for their slowness, and stamping angrily with his wooden leg.

The fleet came. Colonel Nichols, who was in command, took possession of a blockhouse on Staten Island and landed some of his soldiers on Long Island. Then the governor sent a formal demand to know what this behavior might mean. The colonel in reply ordered him to surrender. "Yield peaceably, and I promise freedom and his property to every citizen," he said. Now New Amsterdam had become so well-to-do that many English had come there to live, and of course they preferred to be under the English king. Even the Dutch believed that the company had not treated them fairly, and so they did not feel very unhappy at the thought of having a new ruler. Certainly they would rather live under English rule than have their homes destroyed by English soldiers. The Council urged the governor to surrender, but he said no. The citizens begged him to yield. Still he declared, "I won't surrender."

While they were talking, Colonel Nichols sent another letter, promising that, if they would yield, the trade with Holland should go on as usual, and settlers should come from that country as freely as ever. The governor knew very well that if the people saw that letter they would refuse to fight, so he would not read it to them. A rumor then went through the city, "The English have sent a letter offering good terms," and a crowd gathered around the council room. Even the men who were at work on the defenses dropped their tools and ran crying, "The letter, the letter! Show us the letter!"

"The letter must be read to them," said the Council.

"It shall never be!" roared the governor, pounding the floor with his wooden leg and tearing the letter into pieces.

"Show us the letter!" the crowd still called. The secretary picked up the pieces and put them together, and it was read aloud from the steps of the building.

The governor wrote a strong, manly reply to Colonel Nichols, saying that the Dutch had discovered New Netherland, had bought it of the Indians, had settled upon it; and surely it belonged to them. He trained his guns on the English ships, and he marched down to the landing, ready with his hundred soldiers to fight five or six times that number. The ships had ninety-four guns, and the colonists had about twenty. The gunners on the vessels and the gunners on the land stood waiting the signal to fire. Then a paper was brought to the governor, signed by all the principal citizens, his own son among them, begging him not to allow the destruction of the town. Women crowded about him, weeping and praying him to save their homes. Little children clung to him and cried, "Save us, save us!"

"I would rather be carried out to my grave," cried the dauntless governor; but he was helpless, for the people refused to obey his orders. The white flag of surrender was finally run up, and the governor marched out of the fort at the head of his men with flags flying and drums beating. Down on the shore the English soldiers were already drawn up in line, and soon the English flag was floating over Fort Amsterdam, which now became Fort James. The town had saved its houses, but it had lost its name; it was no longer New Amsterdam, but in honor of the Duke of York it was called New York, and Colonel Nichols became its governor.

Whether the town was English or Dutch, Governor Stuyvesant had no idea of leaving it. He owned a large bowery, or farm, and there he spent his last years. He had fine horses and cattle and the best of fruit trees. He had a prim flower garden laid out in stiff regular beds. Behind the garden was the roomy two-story house to which he delighted to welcome his friends — and among them was his old enemy, Colonel Nichols!

OUTLINE

The Dutch settle in America — the coming of the new governor — his speech — his laws — description of the Dutch houses and gardens — the parlor — the kitchen — social pleasures — the coming of luxuries — the rule of Governor Stuyvesant — startling news from England — fortifying the town — Colonel Nichols's demand — feelings of the citizens — Nichols's second letter — Stuyvesant's refusal to have it read to the people — his reply to Nichols — the citizens' petition — surrender — Stuyvesant and his bowery.

SUGGESTIONS FOR WRITTEN WORK

The coming of Governor Stuyvesant.
A visit to a home in New Amsterdam.
Governor Stuyvesant describes the surrender.

KING PHILIP

CHIEF OF THE WAMPANOAGS

IT will be remembered that before the Pilgrims had been long in Plymouth, Massasoit, chief of the Wampanoags, paid them a visit. He promised to be their friend, and that promise was never broken.

One day a little brown-skinned baby was born in his wigwam. A white mother would have bought her baby a cradle, but an Indian mother would have said, "No, a cradle is not safe, it may tip over. It is heavy, too, and I want to carry my baby with me wherever I go."

So this child, like other Indian children, was rolled
in soft furs and bound to a board a little larger than
himself. A hoop, or a sort of hood, was put up above his
head; and then, even if the board had a hard fall, the
baby was not hurt. Little playthings hung from the
hoop; but he had small need of them, for there were
always so many interesting things to watch.

When his father had gone out to hunt that they might
have food, his mother would go into the forest for wood;
and while she was gathering it, the board and the baby
hung on the branch of a tree. The breeze swayed them
to and fro, the green leaves fluttered and glittered in
the sunshine. The squirrels chattered all around him;
sometimes the birds lighted on the branches near him
and looked curiously to see what kind of bird he was
and what kind of nest that strange cradle could be.
Then when his mother was tired and sat down under
the tree to rest, she sang him songs about the bravest
men of his tribe, how they had saved their people in
time of war and how many of their enemies they had
slain. " By and by, my little Metacomet," she would
say, " you, too, will be a brave fighter. You must lead
your people on the warpath, and you must never yield."

When Metacomet grew older, he found that there
were many things for him to learn. Stories were told
him of deeds of courage, and he must remember them
and be able to tell them again. He must learn to use a

bow and arrow. "You must shoot straight and quickly," his father would say, "and you must not give your enemy a chance to shoot first." He must learn the difference between the footprints made by the moccasins of his own people and those made by other tribes. He

METACOMET LEARNING HIS LESSONS

must learn how to put on the war paint and what the different colors meant. He must learn not to scream when he was frightened or to cry when he was hurt. He must not whine for fire if he was cold or for food if he was hungry. He had no books about plants and animals, but he must learn about them. He must know which roots were good to eat, on which side of the trees the moss grew thickest, how to tell the marks made in the bark of a tree by a bear from those made by a moose, how far a wildcat could spring, and how to escape from a rattlesnake. He must learn to make nooses and snares, to hunt and to fish; not for amusement by any means, but because when he became a man and had a wife and children, they would starve if he could not bring them anything to eat from the forest.

Even in his games the Indian boy was ever learning to be strong and skillful and to make his own way in life. The boys wrestled, they ran races, they had shooting and swimming matches and sham battles. The older people were always interested in these contests. If a boy had won in a swimming race, for instance, some one would be sure to remember that one of his family had been a great swimmer and would say to him, " The brother of your grandfather could swim well. He became a mighty warrior. We will see what you will do." Then the little Indian boy was happy indeed, and he made up his mind to be a greater warrior than any of his family.

So it was that the little son of Massasoit grew up. The white people had come to Massachusetts long before he was born, and he, together with his older brother, Wamsutta, must have gone many a time to their settlements. When Massasoit died, Wamsutta became chief in his father's place, and he, too, was friendly with the people at Plymouth. The Indians had bought guns of the whites before this, and Wamsutta and Metacomet used to go to them to buy powder. They told their Plymouth friends that they would like to have names like those of the white people. Then the Plymouth court chose for them the names of two heroes of ancient times, and declared that Wamsutta should be called Alexander and Metacomet should be called Philip.

The whites never felt as sure of Alexander's friendship as they had felt of his father's; and after a while reports began to come to them which said, " Alexander is friendly with the Narragansetts. Beware! " Massasoit's tribe and the Narragansetts had long been bitter enemies. " If they and Alexander have become friends," thought the whites, " it must be that they are planning to attack us." So they sent to the chief a request to come to Plymouth and explain what this meant. He came, but on the way he was taken sick, and a few days later he died. This sudden illness seemed very mysterious to Philip, and he suspected that his brother had been poisoned.

Philip was now chief of the Wampanoags. Every little while the English heard that he was not their friend. " He said he wanted the land back that his tribe had sold to the white men," declared one. "Many Indians from other tribes are coming to see him," said another, " and they have long councils together." " The young men among the Wampanoags and the Narragansetts want to fight and show themselves as brave as their fathers," said still another.

The colonists talked over these things. Then they asked Philip to make a treaty of peace; but he seems

A FANCIFUL PORTRAIT OF KING PHILIP
By Paul Revere

not to have kept it very well, for three or four years later he was asked to make another. Then he replied proudly, "Your governor is but a subject of King

Charles of England. I shall not treat with a subject. I shall treat of peace only with the king, my brother. When he comes, I am ready."

Philip lived at Mount Hope, and not far from his home was the little village of Swanzey. One day in 1675, men from Swanzey came galloping into Boston for help. "The Indians!" they cried, "the Indians are upon us! They have set fire to two houses in our town!" Then both Boston and Plymouth sent messengers straight to King Philip. "Your men have broken the treaty," they were to say. "Send us the ones who burned those houses, that we may punish them, or there will be war at once!" The men never gave their message to King Philip, for when they came near Swanzey they saw that war had already broken out. The savages had attacked the town, and murdered men, women, and little children.

KING PHILIP'S MARK

Then there was no more delay. Men set out from Boston and Plymouth for Mount Hope, and marched night and day. Philip had no idea that any one would attack him so soon, and he was quietly eating his dinner when the English burst in upon him. He fled, but the English pursued him so closely that one man caught the chief's cap from his head, just as he was running into a swamp, where the English could not follow him.

This was the beginning of fierce war. One place after another was attacked by the Indians. At Brookfield, Massachusetts, there was one large house so much stronger than the others that all the whites crowded into it. The Indians fired through the walls; they tied long poles together with burning rags on the end, and tried to get near enough to set fire to the house. But the bullets of the men within drove them back. They tied the burning rags to arrows, and shot them up into the air, so they would fall on the roof and kindle it; but the people in the garret cut through the roof, and put out the fires. Then they built a rude sort of platform several yards long, put hay, chips, and flax on the end, set the mass afire, and, using a barrel for a wheel, rolled it with long poles toward the house. The Indians were sheltered by the planks, and the bullets of the white men could not touch them. The fire was too large to be put out by throwing water upon it from the windows. "We can do nothing more," groaned the brave defenders. "But see, God himself is coming to our help!" cried one, for a thick cloud was hanging over them, and suddenly a heavy rain began to fall. The fires went out; and before the Indians could make any new attack, soldiers came, and they fled.

The Connecticut River was the "far west" in those

days, and the little villages near its banks were in terrible danger. Springfield, Hatfield, Deerfield, Hadley, and many others were attacked by the savages. A strange story is told of the attack on Hadley. It was a fast day, and all the people were in church. In the midst of the prayer, they heard the awful warwhoop of the Indians. The men rushed out with their guns, but the Indians were here, there, and everywhere; there seemed to be thousands of them. It was all so sudden that for an instant the men were dazed and stood staring and clutching their weapons. One more instant, and the savages would have been upon them. Suddenly a tall, white-bearded man appeared. He had the bearing of a military commander, and in a moment the men of Hadley found themselves obeying his orders. They formed in line, shot, and charged; the Indians ran, and Hadley was saved. They turned back to their leader, but he was gone. " Who was he ? " they asked, but no one had ever seen him before. They never saw him again, and when in after years they told their children of him, they said in hushed and reverent voices, " It was an angel from heaven."

The next that was known of Philip, he and his men attacked the little village of Lancaster. The people there had been told by spies that the Indians meant to burn their town, and they had sent their minister to Boston, thirty-five miles away, to ask for soldiers to

THE MYSTERIOUS VISITOR AT HADLEY

From a painting by F. A. Chapman

protect them. The soldiers were coming, but the Indians came sooner. Just at sunrise the terrible warwhoop was heard. In a few hours the English troops arrived, but the village had been burned, many people killed, and many others carried away as prisoners. Among these was the wife of the minister. "We will not kill her," they said. "She is the wife of the great medicine man of the village. He will pay us well by and by to get her again." They treated her as well as they could, for if she died they would lose the ransom that they hoped to get. Nevertheless, she had a very hard time. At first there was plenty to eat, for they had stolen from Lancaster all that they could carry away. Soon, however, the food gave out, and they had to eat acorns, roots, pounded bones, the bark of trees, and any kind of animal they could catch or shoot. Once she had a feast. Philip's little son, a boy of nine of whom he was very fond, was with him. "Will you make my boy a cap?" he asked his prisoner. "Yes," she replied, and soon the little fellow was strutting about in it. Then the father in payment invited her to dinner, and gave her a pancake "about as big as two fingers." She said afterwards, "It was made of parched wheat, beaten, and fried in bear's grease; but I thought I never tasted pleasanter meat in my life." After three months of this wandering, she was ransomed for about one hundred dollars, and given up to her husband in Boston.

At last Philip was pursued to his old home at Mount Hope. The only way that he could escape by land was by a narrow isthmus, and that the English held. One of the chief's men said to him, "We cannot get away; we must yield." But this unyielding chieftain was so angry that with a single blow of his tomahawk he killed the man who had advised surrender. This man's brother slipped away from his chief and went to the English. "Philip has killed my brother. I can tell you where he is," he said. Without a moment's delay, the English marched upon the hiding-place of the chief. "When he tries to escape, he will have to go by this spot," said the commander, and he ordered an Englishman and the Indian deserter to watch for him. Soon they saw him running at full speed, and both men fired. The white man's gun missed fire, but the Indian's bullet went straight, and the chief fell dead. It would have broken his heart if he had known the fate of his little boy, for the child was sent with hundreds of other captives to the West Indies and sold as a slave. He was the last of the race of Massasoit, the faithful friend of the Englishmen.

OUTLINE

The treatment of little Metacomet — what he learned — his games — Massasoit's sons and the Pilgrims — new names for the Indians — the whites suspect Alexander — his death — why the whites distrusted Philip — the treaty of peace — the attack on Swanzey — the whites march to Mount Hope — the repulse at

Brookfield — the commander at Hadley — A prisoner among the Indians — death of Philip — fate of his son.

SUGGESTIONS FOR WRITTEN WORK

Metacomet and a white boy tell each other what they have to learn.

The two boys describe their games.

A Brookfield colonist describes the Indian attack.

THE MEN WHO EXPLORED THE MISSISSIPPI

IN 1675, at the time of King Philip's War, there were colonies in all the states bordering on the Atlantic from Maine to South Carolina, and they were all subject to England. Most of the French settlements were on the St. Lawrence River and the Great Lakes. The Indians had told the French of a mighty stream to the southward; and whenever a group of Frenchmen were sitting around the fire some long evening in the little village of Montreal, some one was sure to ask, "Where do you suppose the Mississippi River empties?"

"The men who went with the Spaniard De Soto declared that it emptied into the Gulf of Mexico," one would reply. Another would retort, "That tale is a hundred years old. De Soto went off on a wild-goose chase to search for gold. He did not find any, and of course his men had to tell some big story when they came back." Then another would say more thoughtfully, " The Indians who live to the west of us declare that far to the west of them are strange people who have no beards. They must be Chinese, and I believe that the Mississippi flows into the Pacific Ocean. What fortunes we could make if we could only find that river and trade with China ! "

" Who knows whether there is any river ? " another would demand laughingly. " The Indians talk about ' big water,' but who can tell whether they mean a great river or the ocean ? "

There was a young man named Robert la Salle who was so much interested in this mysterious stream that he thought of it by day and dreamed of it by night. At last he made up his mind to go in search of it. He had little money to pay for canoes and provisions and presents for the Indians through whose country he must pass, but he owned some land eight or nine miles from Montreal. So he sold it and started on his exploring trip. Through the forest and down the Ohio he made his way. Then his men refused to go any farther, and he had to return to Canada. Every one laughed at him. " There 's the man who went to China," they said. They pointed out the land that he had sold, saying, " There 's La Salle's China," or *La Chine*, as it is in French.

Even though this expedition had failed, it made people think more about the unknown river, and finally Governor Frontenac determined to send explorers in search of it. The men whom he chose were Louis Joliet, a fur trader, and Father Marquette, a priest. All that the two men did to prepare for their long journey was to buy two birch-bark canoes, some smoked meat, and Indian corn. Five men were engaged to go with them, and they set out. They hoped to find Indians to show them the way; and surely they needed guides, for their only map was one that they had drawn as best they could from the stories of the red men.

They went west as far as Green Bay, at the northern end of Lake Michigan. The Indians who lived there were friendly. After they had feasted the strangers, they asked, " Where are you going, Frenchmen? "

" We are going to find the great river, the Mississippi," they replied.

" O Frenchmen," the Indians pleaded, " do not go there. The tribes whose wigwams are on the banks of that river are terrible. They kill every one who comes near them. There is an evil spirit, too, that lives in a great gulf of waters, and he will drag you down into his den."

" We are Christians," replied Marquette, " and evil spirits cannot hurt Christians."

" There are two dreadful monsters that stay on a

great rock beside the river," continued the Indians.
" They will eat you and your canoes."

" Not when we show them this," replied Marquette,
holding his crucifix high up before the red men. " If
you will listen to me, I will tell you how you may go
among monsters and not be harmed." Then he told

THE DISCOVERY OF THE MISSISSIPPI BY MARQUETTE
From a painting by J. N. Marchand

them about the religion of Christ and taught them to
say a prayer.

The explorers said good-by and went on their way.
Soon they came to another little Indian village. In the

midst of the cluster of wigwams stood a great cross. Furs and bows and arrows and red belts were hanging on it. "What does that mean?" Joliet asked.

"The cross belongs to the God of the Frenchmen," the Indians replied. "We heard of him from a Black Robe like you," and they turned to Marquette. "We had plenty of food last winter, and so we have given him offerings because we are grateful. But where are you going?"

"My friend, the Black Robe, is going to tell the Indians about God," answered Joliet, "and I am going to search for the Mississippi River and explore new countries so I can tell our governor at home about them. Will you give us guides to show us the way?"

"Yes," they cried, and soon the Frenchmen had left the little village far behind them.

At last they were in the "big water," the mighty river that they had come to discover. Every night they ran their canoes ashore, built a fire, and slept. Every day they floated onward. It was a wonderful country that they were passing through. June had come, and everything was fresh and bright. There were beautiful groves, dense forests, prairies, cliffs, and great masses of tangled grapevines. There were flowers of all colors. Buffaloes and deer and many other animals stared at them from the river banks. Strange fishes bumped against their canoes. One morning when they were near the shore, one of the company cried suddenly, "See, those are men's footprints there in the mud!" "And that is surely a path," said another. "It must lead to an Indian village." "We will go and see," declared the two leaders. After they had walked up the path for nearly six miles, they caught sight of a group of wigwams. They shouted so that the Indians might know they were coming as friends and not trying to surprise them. In ·a moment the whole village, men, women, and children, had run out of doors to see who had come. Four tall, dignified men came toward the explorers, holding up two peace pipes. That meant, "Let us be friends," and so they all walked together into the village. The chief made a speech of welcome, and after that the whole company of Indians escorted the strangers to another village where a greater chief lived. Then there was speechmaking indeed. The second chief told them the sun shone brighter and the whole earth was more beautiful because they had come. "You have even made our river calm," he declared, "for your canoes removed the rocks as you came." There was a feast, of course, and then the travelers went away.

When they had floated on to where the city of Alton, Illinois, now stands, they looked up on a high cliff, and there were the monsters that the Indians had told them about. These monsters were figures painted on the rock. Their faces were a little like those of men, but their bodies were scaly and ended like the tails of fish. They had horns and fiery red eyes. A little farther on, the Frenchmen heard the roar of the evil spirit that they had been told about. That was made by the water rushing among the rocks in a little bay. Then they came to the mouth of the Missouri, and there they found something worse than painted monsters to be afraid of, for the river plunged so madly into the Mississippi that the little canoes were tossed and whirled about and almost overturned in the flood.

Still the explorers went on till they had come to where the Arkansas Indians lived. "You'd better not go any farther," said they. "There are tribes to the south of us who will kill you. They do not shoot with bows and arrows, but with fire-sticks like yours that they have bought of the Spaniards." The French leaders talked together about what was best to do. "We may be sure that the river empties into the Gulf of Mexico," they said. "If we go on any farther, we shall certainly be captured by the Indians or the Spaniards. Let us go back to Canada and tell the governor what we have seen." It was a hard journey, for now there was no easy floating, but instead many hundred miles of paddling upstream. For eleven weeks they toiled, and at last they were again at Green Bay. Marquette was ill and could not go any farther for a long while, but

Joliet went on and told Governor Frontenac of all the wonders they had seen.

Of course La Salle was much interested in Joliet's report, and a few years later he had a plan to propose to the governor. "Let us build a line of forts along the Mississippi," he said, "and put a strong colony at its mouth. Then neither the Spanish nor the English can buy furs of the Indians along the river. France will have all that fur trade, and we ourselves shall become rich men."

La Salle went to France to ask the king for leave to build forts, and the king told him he might build as many as he chose. As soon as he came back, he made ready for a journey to the mouth of the Mississippi. "Will you go with us?" he asked a number of Indians.

"Yes," was the answer, "but braves do not cook. We must have our squaws to cook for us."

"The squaws may go," La Salle agreed.

"But they will not go without their children," declared the Indians.

So it was that between fifty and sixty persons, white men, red men, women, and children, set off. Joliet had gone in the spring, but now it was the depth of winter, and until they reached the place where St. Louis now stands, they had to drag their canoes and provisions on sledges over the ice and snow. Glad enough they were when at last they could get into their boats and float down the stream. Once they were badly startled. A dense fog had set in. They were close to the shore, when suddenly they heard loud yells and the beating of an Indian drum. "That means a war dance," said the explorers. "Let us cross to the other side." They crossed, and worked with all their might to build a rude fort of logs for fear the savages would attack them. All in a moment the fog cleared away, and across the river they saw the Indians, who stood listening to the strange sounds and wondering what they could be. These Indians were all ready to be friendly. Another tribe showed La Salle a most unusual honor, for, as he was not well, the chief himself came in all state to visit the white man. The master of ceremonies walked first, followed by six tall Indians to make sure that the way was clear. Then came two men carrying great fans of white feathers, and one man with a broad copper disk that shone and gleamed in the sunshine. After all these the chief appeared, dressed in a fine white blanket. He and La Salle made speeches to each other. La Salle presented knives, beads, red cloth, and mirrors; and the little procession turned about and went gravely away.

At last the explorers came to the mouth of the river. The Indian braves and the squaws and the children must have been greatly amazed at the next move, for all the Frenchmen took their stand with their guns. They chanted the *Te Deum*, "We praise Thee, O God," and

LA SALLE TAKING POSSESSION OF THE MISSISSIPPI VALLEY
From a painting by J. N. Marchand

some other Latin hymns. The guns were fired. La Salle
stepped into the centre of the group and planted a tall
post on which was written, " Louis the Great, King of
France and Navarre, April 9, 1682." He made a long
speech, declaring that he claimed for his sovereign all
the land that was drained by the Mississippi and by all
the rivers that flow into it. " Long live the king!" the
men shouted, " Long live the king! " Again there was
firing of guns. Then a great cross was set up near the
post, and at its foot was buried a leaden plate on which

the arms of France were engraved. Another Latin hymn was sung. That was all; but it was because of this little ceremony on the lonely shore of the Gulf of Mexico that France claimed as her own all the land between the Alleghanies and the Rocky Mountains.

La Salle did not give up the rest of his plan, — to found a colony at the mouth of the Mississippi. Not long after his return to Canada he went to France. Wonderful stories had gone before him. "Louisiana is full of peaches and plums and berries of all sorts," they said. "There are all kinds of trees. The soil is so rich that if you only scratch the surface of the ground, you can raise whatever you choose to plant."

" I 'd like to go there to live," said one after another. When La Salle went back, eight or ten families went with him. They did not go by Canada, but sailed directly for the Gulf of Mexico.

The rest of the story is a sad one. The pilots made a mistake and went four hundred miles beyond the mouth of the Mississippi. The food ship and one other vessel were lost. Sickness set in, and more than a hundred men died within a few days. The others would gladly have gone back to France, but only one ship was left, and that was not large enough to carry them all across the ocean. La Salle set out on foot for Canada to get help, a terrible undertaking. On the way he was murdered by some of his own men. The lonely colonists met a cruel fate, for some of them were killed by the Indians, and the others were made prisoners by the Spaniards.

Such was the end of La Salle's attempt to start a colony at the mouth of the Mississippi. The colony was finally founded, and was called New Orleans; but this was after La Salle had been dead for many years.

OUTLINE

The English and the French colonies in 1675 — " Where does the Mississippi empty ? " — La Salle's journey down the Ohio — Governor Frontenac sends Joliet and Marquette to find the Mississippi — the Indians urge them not to go — the cross in the Indian village — they come to the " big water " — the shores of the Mississippi — a visit to the Indian chiefs — the monsters on the cliff — the evil spirit — the mouth of the Missouri — the warning of the Arkansas Indians — the return of the explorers — La Salle's plan for forts and a colony — the king's permission — La Salle's preparations — the journey to St. Louis — a war dance — the chief's visit — the ceremonies at the mouth of the Mississippi — La Salle tries to found a colony — its troubles and its fate — murder of La Salle.

SUGGESTIONS FOR WRITTEN WORK

A Frenchman tells his family why he wishes to go to Louisiana. What Joliet told Governor Frontenac of his journey.

One of the Indians describes the greatest danger that the explorers met.

WILLIAM PENN

WHO FOUNDED PENNSYLVANIA

WHILE La Salle was on the Mississippi River planning a colony that failed, an English Quaker, named William Penn, was getting ready to found a colony that was to succeed. Long before this the Quakers had thought of America. " The Puritans have gone to Massachusetts," they said, "and the Roman Catholics have gone to Maryland. Why should not we have a home of our own in the New World ? " A number of Quakers crossed the ocean and made little settlements on the banks of the Delaware. Penn said to himself, " What a glorious thing it would be if we could have a country where not only Quakers but every one else could worship God as he thought right! " At last he planned a way in which this might be brought about. King Charles had owed Penn's father a large sum of money, so the young man asked, " Friend Charles, wilt thou give me land in America instead of that money ? " The king was more than willing. Land in America was of no great value, he believed, and so he readily gave Penn a piece almost as large as the whole of England. " It shall be called New Wales," said Penn; but the king had the good taste not to like this name. " Then let it be Sylvania," Penn suggested. " Pennsylvania," declared the quick-witted king. Penn thought that might look as if he wished to honor himself, but the king said, " Oh no, it is to honor the admiral, your father." So Pennsylvania — Penn's woodland — was written on the maps of the new state.

Just where his settlement was to be, he did not know, but he sent three men across the ocean to find a good place and treat with the Indians. The town was to be named Philadelphia, or the City of Brotherly Love. He had a de-

WILLIAM PENN

lightful time planning it. He did not mean to have the houses dropped down anywhere and to have the streets wriggle and twist to go by the houses. His town was to have streets running north and south, cut at right angles by other streets running east and west. Those that went north and south were to be numbered, First Street, Second Street, and so on; those that went east and west were to be named for the trees of the forest, —

Chestnut, Walnut, Spruce, and Pine. The river banks
were never to be built upon, but always to be open
to the people. The streets were made narrow because
Penn was not planning for a large city but for a " green
country town." He marked on his plan just where the
city hall was to be, where he meant to have open parks,
and where his own house was to stand. He wrote a
friendly letter to the English and the Swedes who were
already settled on his land, telling them he hoped they
would not dislike having him as governor, for they
should be treated fairly and make whatever laws they
thought best. He also wrote to the Indians that he was
their friend and that he wanted to live with them in
love and peace. He sent his cousin across the ocean to
deliver these letters and act as governor until he himself could come. Then he set to work and wrote a busi-
nesslike advertisement. It told how much it would cost
to cross the ocean, how much he would sell land for,
what kind of country Pennsylvania was, and what things
colonists would need. It was not long before ships
began to carry settlers to Pennsylvania. It is thought
that three thousand came the first year.

These settlers, even the earliest of them, had none of
the hard times that the people of Plymouth and Jamestown had to endure. Of course there were no houses;
and when the first ship sailed up the beautiful Delaware
River, her passengers had to scramble up the bank and

shelter themselves as best they could until their houses were built. Some of them made huts of bark. Some dug into the river bank and beat down the earth for floors. For walls they piled up sods, or they cut down branches and small trees and set them up around the floor. For chimneys, they mixed grass and clay together. Some of them drove forked sticks into the ground, laid a pole in the crotches, and hung a kettle on the pole. A fire was built under it, and there the cooking was done. It was a busy time, for while all this was going on, the surveyors were marking off lots as fast as they could. The settlers were in a hurry, for they wanted to build their houses. Some made them of logs, and some had brought the frames with them, each piece marked and numbered, so they could be put up very quickly. The Indians were much interested. They gazed with wonder at a wooden house growing almost as rapidly as a wigwam. They often did more than gaze; they helped those who were in need. On the voyage a man had died, and his widow, with eight or nine children, found herself alone in a strange country. The white people, busy as they were, saw that she had a cave-house at once, and the Indians hurried to bring venison and corn for her and her little family.

The next year, in 1682, Penn himself came to America. He landed first at Newcastle, and there he took formal possession of his land in the old English fashion; that

is, he took a cup of water, a handful of soil, a bit of
turf, and a twig. When he saw his new town, he was delighted. The situation, the air, the water, the sky, —
everything pleased him, and he wrote his friends most
enthusiastic letters. He told them about the nuts and
grapes and wheat, about the wild pigeons, the big tur-
keys, the ducks, and the geese, all free to whoever chose
to shoot them. The water was full of fish and the forest
abounded with deer. It is no wonder that settlers hurried to Pennsylvania.

Of course the Indians were eager to see the new
governor, and very likely a group of them stood on the
bank when he first landed. He was quite as eager to
meet them, and soon they came together for feasting
and a treaty of peace. Penn was exceedingly handsome. His hair was long and lay on his shoulders in
curls, as was the fashion of the day. His clothes had
not the silver trimmings and the lace that most young
men of wealth were used to wear, but he liked to have
them of rich material and well made. " He was the
handsomest, best-looking, and liveliest of gentlemen,"
declared a lady who saw him at that time. Tradition
says that he and the Indians met under a great elm that
stood on the river bank. The deep blue stream was
flowing softly by, the blue sky was overhead, the leaves
of the elm were gently fluttering, and little birds were
peering down curiously between the branches. The

PENN'S TREATY WITH THE INDIANS

chief seated himself for a council. His wisest men sat close behind him in a half circle. Behind them sat the younger braves. Penn stood before them and told them about his colony. He said that he wished to be a good friend to the Indians and to treat them kindly. As each sentence was translated to them, they gave a shout of pleasure. At the end they said, "We will never do any wrong to you or your friends;" and Penn declared, "We will live in love as long as the sun gives light." Penn paid the Indians for their land just as the settlers of Massachusetts, Rhode Island, and New Netherland had done. He gave them cloth, bells, guns, kettles, axes, scissors, knives, mirrors, shoes, beads, combs, and shirts. Of course all these things together would hardly buy a rod of land in Philadelphia to-day; but they were of great value to the Indians, and they were well pleased with the bargain. They were also well pleased with the governor. He was dignified and courtly in his bearing; but when he spoke to them, he was simple and friendly. He would sit with them and eat of their hominy

BELT OF WAMPUM GIVEN TO PENN
The Indian and White Man clasp hands in friendship

and roasted acorns as if he were one of them. At college he had been fond of outdoor sports, and there is a story that once when the red men were leaping to show what they could do, he suddenly stepped out and

leaped higher and farther than they. The Indians were
delighted. " He is a great man," they said, " but when
he comes among us, he is our brother." They called him
" Onas," the Indian word for pen or quill. " Onas always does what he says he will do," they told the other
tribes.

Penn stayed two years in America, but not all the
time in Philadelphia. Once he went to Maryland to have
a talk with Lord Baltimore about boundaries. America
was so large, and a few miles of wilderness seemed of
so little value, that the English kings gave away broad
slices of the country without taking much trouble to
make sure that no two men had the same piece. Lord
Baltimore claimed the very land on which Philadelphia
had been settled. It became known that he was on his
way to England to lay his claim before the king. Then
Penn had to cross the ocean to defend his grant. He
expected to return soon, but one trouble after another
kept him in England for fifteen years.

At last the time came when he and his wife and children could come to Philadelphia. He built a fine brick
house at a place which he named Pennsbury, twenty
miles up the river. It was handsomely furnished. There
were dishes of silver and china, plush couches, embroidered chairs, satin curtains, and a heavy carpet—perhaps
the first one that ever came across the ocean. There were
gardens, made beautiful not only with plants brought

from England, but with wild flowers of America. Lawns
and terraces ran down to the river bank. There was a
stable for twelve horses, there was a " coach and four,"
there was a barge to be rowed by six oarsmen. The Indians came freely to visit him, and he entertained them
on his lawn or in the great hall of his handsome house.
He roamed over the country on horseback, and was once
lost in the woods near Valley Forge as completely as if
he had not been on his own ground. Once when he
was riding to meeting, he came up with a child who
was also going to the same place. The shy little bare-
foot girl must have been half afraid but much delighted
when the governor caught her up, set her behind him
on his great horse, and trotted on to meeting with her.
It would be pleasant if we could think of Penn as spending the rest of his days in the country life that he enjoyed; but he had been in America only two years when
he was obliged to return to England. Never again did
he see beautiful Pennsbury, his Indian friends, the city
that he loved, or the smoothly flowing Delaware.

OUTLINE

The Quaker colonies — Penn's plan for a colony — a royal grant
— his plan for the city — his letters to the settlers on his land
and to the Indians — his advertisement — the shelter of the first
settlers in Philadelphia — the first houses — kindness of the Indians — the coming of Penn — his letters home — the welcome
of the Indians — Penn's appearance — the treaty of friendship —

Penn's payment to the Indians — his behavior to them — what they thought of him — Penn's journey to Maryland — he leaves America — his return — Pennsbury — stories of Penn.

SUGGESTIONS FOR WRITTEN WORK

A settler describes his first days in Philadelphia.
Penn writes his wife about Pennsylvania.
An Indian tells a distant tribe about Penn.

GEORGE WASHINGTON

THE YOUNG SOLDIER

IT would seem as if a few groups of colonists might live in peace together when they had a whole continent on which to choose places for their homes; but during the half century following the settlement of Philadelphia there was a great deal of fighting in America. Much of it was caused by the fact that whenever England, France, and Spain were at war, their colonies also fought. After a while, however, the colonists of England and France had a quarrel of their own. Its occasion was the land along the Ohio River. This message came to the French: "Those Englishmen are planning to send out settlers to the Ohio."

"That will not do," declared the French. "We want to be able to float down the Ohio into the Mississippi, and so on to the Gulf of Mexico. La Salle explored the Ohio. Moreover, we discovered the Mississippi, and the Ohio flows into it; therefore the Ohio is ours."

The English laughed at this. " The French claim all the rivers that flow into the Mississippi ! " they cried. " They might as well claim all the countries that drink French brandy."

Both nations knew that a strong fort built at the point where the Allegheny joins the Monongahela would hold the river, for no enemies could sail by such a fortification. Governor Duquesne of Canada began quietly to build forts, each one a little nearer this spot. Governor Dinwiddie of Virginia was wide awake and keeping a close watch on the doings of the French. When he heard that a third fort had been begun, he said to himself, " That has gone far enough. I will send some one to warn them that this land belongs to us."

It was not easy to choose a messenger. The governor thought it over. " It is a hard journey," he said to himself. " There will be ice and snow and Indians and all sorts of dangers. We must have a man who knows how to make his way through the forest and will not be afraid of difficulties. That young surveyor who has done so much work for Lord Fairfax is a good woodsman. He is cool and sensible, and whatever he undertakes he does well. He is not the man to be imposed upon, either; and even if those smooth Frenchmen treat him as if he were the king of France, he will not forget what he was sent

THE YOUNG SURVEYOR

for." There was something else to be careful about. " It won't do to send any rude, blunt messenger," thought the governor. " Such a fellow would get us into a fight in three days. This young Washington knows how to behave in a parlor as well as in the forest. The young-ster is only twenty-one, but I believe he is the man to go."

Then the governor sent for the young man and told him what was needed. He set out with a little company of white men and Indians. The mountains were covered with snow, and the cold November rains were falling.

Drip, drip, came the water from the branches as the men pushed on in Indian file through the wilderness. For two weeks it either rained or snowed, and it was always cold and wet. The wind blew upon them in tempests whenever they left the shelter of the forest. The heavy rains had swollen the brooks to creeks, and the creeks to rivers; but, large or small, they must all be crossed.

At last Washington saw through the trees the gleam of the French flag and smoke rising from a chimney. This was the nearest of the three forts, though it was hardly a fort as yet. The French were most polite to their English visitors; but they were exceedingly careful not to say a word that would show what their plans were. " The commander is at Fort Le Bœuf," they said, " and the reply must come from him. It is time for supper now; come and eat with us." At supper they drank a good deal of wine, and then they forgot their caution. "We are going to have the Ohio," they declared; and went on good naturedly, " Of course you can raise two men to our one, but your English are slow folk. We can build our forts and take the whole country while you are getting ready." Washington did not boast about what the English could do, but he wrote all this carefully in his journal to show to Governor Dinwiddie.

The next day he went on to Fort Le Bœuf. He presented the governor's letter, which reminded the French

that they were on land belonging to the English. The
commander replied, " I will send the letter to Governor

WASHINGTON ON HIS MISSION TO THE OHIO

Duquesne; but this is where he has placed me, and here
I must stay until he sends me somewhere else."

Washington took his leave. The horses went so slowly
through the snow that, to save time, he returned on foot

with only one man. The coming had been hard enough, but the return was much worse. The cold had become more intense; the rivers were full of floating ice. Washington was knocked off the raft into ten feet of bitterly cold water, and had to spend that night on a little island without fire or shelter. There was danger from the Indians, and more than once he was fired upon by them; but he came out safely from all dangers and gave Governor Dinwiddie the French commander's reply.

"We must get ahead of them," declared the governor. "We will build a fort just where the Allegheny joins the Monongahela, and we will hold the Ohio." So he sent men there to build the fort; but the French drove them away, and in high glee built a fortification of their own which they named for the governor, Fort Duquesne. Governor Dinwiddie had sent another band of men to help the first, with Washington at its head. He heard that the French had driven the first colonists away and were coming to attack his company. With his few men he could not meet them, so he went back a little way to wait for more troops.

It was not long before a few militiamen and fifty regular soldiers came. Their captain put on a great many airs because his regulars were paid by the king. "We belong to the king's army," he declared, "and the king's soldiers do not take orders from a young fellow in the colonial militia." His men followed their captain's lead

and refused to help make a road or drag the cannon.
They were soon frightened into helping, however, for
the scouts told them that the French were coming upon
them. Then they forgot that they were taking orders
from a colonial major and worked as hard as they could
to help make an intrenchment, dig a ditch, and cut down
trees for breastworks. The French came upon them,
twice as many as the colonists. The fight lasted for nine
hours. The powder gave out and the provisions gave
out. There was nothing to be gained by lying down
behind the logs and starving ; so Washington surrendered. The French were jubilant. They had driven off
the English and they held the Ohio.

But somehow the English would not stay driven off.
At length the king of England began to find out that
the French were trying to crowd his colonies into a little strip of land near the coast, and that if he expected
to have any more than that he must fight. Then he
sent General Braddock to Virginia with one thousand
men.

Long before the vessel came to the wharf, the colonists could see the red coats of the soldiers. The regulars were with them, and they were delighted. Braddock
made Washington one of his officers, but he had no idea
of listening to his advice. Washington was much troubled. " The general knows how to fight the French,"
he thought, " but he seems to think that the Indians will

march out in line like white men." So he told him respectfully how the Indians behaved in a fight. "They hide behind rocks and trees," he said, " and there will be a storm of bullets when no one is in sight."

"Regulars know how to return bullets," replied Braddock. " It would be a strange thing if British troops could not meet a handful of naked Indians."

The line of redcoats and of colonial soldiers set out on the long hard march through the forest. They crossed the Monongahela. They were climbing a hill when suddenly shots began to come from all directions and the forest echoed with the yells of the Indians. The French were in front, the Indians were on both sides, but hidden behind trees. The regulars were so dazed at this new kind of fighting that they ran like sheep. The colonists had learned how to meet Indians, and so they hid behind trees and returned the fire. Even then Braddock could not see that there was any other way to fight than the one he had learned, and he shouted to his men to come out and form in line. Of course the only end to such a battle was the wild retreat of the English. Cannon, provisions, food, arms, clothes, horses, and money were forgotten in the mad rush for safety. Braddock was mortally wounded and soon died. When the fugitives dared to stop, he was buried in the forest, and wagons were rolled over his grave lest the Indians should find it.

It was owing chiefly to Washington's skill and coolness that any of the men escaped. Four bullets were shot through his coat, but he was not hurt. Afterwards an Indian chief said, " He will never die in battle. I told all my braves to aim at him, but they could not hit him." If the Indian had known what severe fighting lay before the young officer, he might not have been so sure that Washington would never die in battle.

OUTLINE

Why the colonies fought — Governor Duquesne builds forts — Governor Dinwiddie's warning — choosing a messenger — Washington's journey through the forest — he is entertained at the French fort — the Frenchmen's boast — Washington at Fort Le Bœuf — his return to Virginia — Governor Dinwiddie attempts to build a fort — Washington is sent to help the builders — the coming of the militia and the regulars — the attack of the French — General Braddock comes to Virginia — Washington warns Braddock — Braddock's reply — Braddock is conquered and slain — Washington's escape.

SUGGESTIONS FOR WRITTEN WORK

Governor Dinwiddie tells Washington what he is to do on his mission to the French.

Washington's report of the journey.

A colonial soldier describes Braddock's defeat.

JAMES WOLFE

WHO CAPTURED QUEBEC

AFTER Braddock's defeat at the Monongahela, the French gained battle after battle. Then they began to lose and the English to win. There was only one thing which could end the war, and that was the capture of Quebec. So long as the French held the city on the rock, they could laugh at the attempts of the English to conquer Canada ; and so long as they held the city, the English would never give up trying to capture it.

This was what an Englishman named William Pitt was saying to himself. He was prime minister of England, and therefore he had to make plans for the war and choose the men to carry them out. " Quebec must be taken," he thought, " and James Wolfe can take it if any one can."

Wolfe had been a soldier ever since he was a boy of fifteen. He was so earnest and so eager to succeed that some one once said to the king, " That young Wolfe is mad."

" Mad, is he ? " the king growled. " Then I only hope he will bite some of my generals."

Before long, Montcalm, who was in command at Quebec, heard that the English were coming. " They can never get up the river without pilots," he said ; but he was too good a soldier not to make ready to receive them in case they did get through the zigzag channel. Quebec stood high and safe on the great rocky promontory.

JAMES WOLFE

Below it was the St. Charles River, flowing into the St. Lawrence. Beyond the St. Charles was a steep bank which stretched along the St. Lawrence for seven or eight miles. Montcalm chained heavy logs together and fastened this "boom" across the St. Charles so no ships

could sail up the stream and attack the city from the rear.
He stationed his forces along the steep bank. He built
earthworks and batteries to make sure that Wolfe could
not land at that place. Then he waited. After a long
while the English ships were seen. " They cannot get up
to the Isle of Orleans," declared the French, and they
crowded to the shore to see them run upon the rocks.
Behold, the ships sailed on as easily as if they were in
a mill pond. That was no wonder, for the English had
captured some French pilots and had said to them, " You
are to steer these vessels up the river ; and if one runs
aground, you will be hanged." Of course every vessel
went through the channel safely, and the men were
landed on the Isle of Orleans. Wolfe walked to the farther end of the island, and stood looking at Quebec only
three or four miles away. There was the Lower Town,
that is, the houses on the flats near the river. Above
that was the Upper Town with its green trees and gray
stone buildings. Still higher was the citadel, and around
it was a thick stone wall wherever the cliffs were not
protection enough. Batteries were everywhere with
their guns pointing toward the river, and Wolfe must
have felt almost discouraged when he saw them. Then
he looked below the town. There was the St. Charles
guarded by the boom of logs. Beyond it were the steep
banks, and along these banks thousands of French soldiers were encamped.

Wolfe did not know what to do, but Montcalm knew
precisely what *he* would do. "Wolfe cannot land within
seven or eight miles of the city," he thought, "and there
is no use in my going out to meet him. Let him stay
until his provisions begin to give out, and then he will go
home. If he stays a little too long, the frost will catch
him and he will be frozen into the river as tight as a
rat in a trap." The governor of the town, however,
wanted to make one effort to destroy the fleet. He made
his arrangements; then he climbed up into the steeple of
a church and stood there in the darkness watching the
river to see what would happen.

A little while before midnight the English soldiers
saw black, vague shapes coming slowly toward them.
Suddenly there were explosions, tongues of fire, sheets
of flame. Missiles hissed and screamed and roared and
shrieked; muskets and cannon and bombs exploded;
shot rattled away among the leaves like hailstones.
These were the governor's fireships, coming to burn the
English fleet. Fortunately for the English, they had been
set afire too soon and were nowhere near the fleet. The
English sailors sprang into their boats, caught hold of
the monsters with grappling irons, and towed them to
the shore. There they spluttered and fizzed awhile, and
then burned out harmlessly. The governor climbed down
from the steeple and went back to the camp in the dark,
strangely surprised at the failure of his plan, and won-

dering what the king of France would say about his spending so much money for nothing.

It was June when Wolfe went to Canada. The summer was going swiftly. June had passed; July was almost gone. Still Wolfe thought and planned, but he could not find any way to conquer Montcalm. He had fired hundreds of shells into the town, he had destroyed many buildings; but that was not taking Quebec. He must meet Montcalm in battle and conquer him, and Montcalm would not be met. "The wary old fellow avoids battle," Wolfe wrote to his mother. "But he shall fight," he said to himself; and he determined to land his men on the shore below the St. Charles close to Montcalm's intrenchments, make a dash up the bank, and force the French to meet him.

Now the soldiers had been waiting week after week, and they were half wild with eagerness and impatience. "Why don't we do something?" they had grumbled. When the first companies of these men were put ashore, they forgot that they ought to wait for orders or for the other troops, they forgot that they had a commander, they forgot everything except that the enemy were before them. So they began to scramble up the bank. Of course the French came out then. Their volleys alone would have been enough to drive the few Englishmen away; but a storm suddenly burst upon them, and in a moment the bank was so slippery that no one could climb it.

LANDING OF THE BRITISH TROOPS ABOVE QUEBEC

There was nothing to do but to retreat. The French were delighted. " The war is as good as ended," they declared. Wolfe was almost in despair.

Before Wolfe came to Canada, he had thought that he could go up the river beyond Quebec, land his troops on some level fields known as the Plains of Abraham, and attack the city from that side. But when he saw the place, he found that the Plains of Abraham were a high plateau whose bank was as nearly perpendicular as a bank of earth could be. Still, every other attempt had failed, and September had come. Wolfe determined to try this plan as a last hope. Up the river, beyond the city, went the English warships, though the guns of Quebec bellowed and thundered at them as they passed. " They mean to try to land somewhere," thought Montcalm, and he sent men to prevent them.

They did mean to land somewhere, but it was in the very place where Montcalm had felt sure that no one could land. One dark night sixteen hundred English soldiers got into the small boats and floated gently down the river toward the town. Wolfe and some of his officers were together in one boat. A little while before, Wolfe had received letters from home, and in one of them was a beautiful poem that had recently been published, describing rural scenes and the lives of country people. It is known as Gray's "Elegy." In the midst of his preparations for battle, lines of this poem kept coming into Wolfe's mind, and in the boat that night he began, —

"The curfew tolls the knell of parting day,"

and repeated the stanzas softly to his officers. "Gentlemen," he said, "I would rather have written those lines than take Quebec to-morrow."

They floated on silently, but nearer and nearer the shore. "Who is there?" rang out the voice of a French sentinel.

"France."

"What is your regiment?"

"The Queen's."

This conversation was in French, and the sentinel never suspected that a Scotchman, who knew the language, was answering his questions. A little later another sentinel cried, "Who is there?" and the Scotchman replied, " Provision boats. Hush, the English will hear us ! " So again they were allowed to pass. They came to shore at the foot of the precipice. The Scotchman and twenty-three others had volunteered to go first. " If you can climb it, the rest of the men may follow," said Wolfe. He sat in the boat listening, but not a sound could he hear save the ripple of the river. Suddenly guns were fired at the top of the bank, and the soldiers leaped from the boats and tore their way up the steep. Even here the careful Montcalm had left a small force of men, but they were taken by surprise and easily captured.

Wolfe had left some of his soldiers below the city, and they had pretended to be about to attack Montcalm in his intrenchments. While the French were watching for them, a man came up at full gallop. " The English, the English ! " he cried, " they are on the Plains of Abraham ! " Montcalm spurred his horse, and in three hours he had his thousands of soldiers drawn up on the Plains only half a mile from the English lines. The French dashed forward, shouting and firing, but not an Englishman stirred. When the French were forty yards away, " Fire ! " shouted the English commanders, and such a volley blazed out as few armies have to meet. This was the beginning, and the whole battle was hardly more than a beginning, it was so swift and so soon ended. The English had conquered. " But where is

the general?" demanded the men. The word went
from line to line, "The general is killed," and all their
rejoicing was turned into sorrow. Wolfe had been
wounded three times. At the third blow he fell.

"Shall I get a surgeon?" asked one of his men.

"No, it is all over," he replied, and closed his eyes.

The wild retreat had begun, and an officer cried,
"See how they run!"

That cry aroused the dying general. "Who run?"
he demanded.

"The enemy! they give way everywhere!" was the
reply.

"God be praised!" he said. "I shall die in peace."
And these were the last words of the eager soldier
whose life had been passed in war.

Another brave general was also struck by a fatal
ball. "How long have I to live?" Montcalm asked the
surgeon. "Not more than twelve hours," was the reply.
"So much the better," said the wounded man. "I am
happy that I shall not live to see the surrender of
Quebec."

So it was that Quebec and Canada fell into the hands
of the English, and with it all the land claimed by the
French east of the Mississippi. When the treaty was
signed, France was obliged to give up all her posses-
sions in America except two little islands in the Gulf
of St. Lawrence.

OUTLINE

William Pitt's plan — Wolfe's character — what Montcalm
thought of Pitt's plan — preparations to defend Quebec — Wolfe
comes up the river — he looks at Quebec — Montcalm will not
fight — the governor's attempt to destroy the English fleet —
Wolfe's summer — he tries to force a battle — his retreat — he
concludes to adopt his first plan to attack the city — sails up the
river — floats down at night — recites Gray's "Elegy" — the
sentinels' challenges — the surprise — the news carried to Montcalm — the battle — death of the generals — result of this victory.

SUGGESTIONS FOR WRITTEN WORK

Pitt tells Wolfe his plan.

Wolfe describes Quebec and its defenses.

A French soldier describes the attempt of the English to climb
up the slippery bank below the town.

WHEN PONTIAC BESIEGED DETROIT

AFTER Wolfe had captured Quebec, and the Al-
gonquin Indians had found that the English had
become the rulers of Canada, they were much troubled.
"There is no one to help us now," they said. "The
Iroquois will attack us and the English settlers will
take our lands. What shall we do?"

A wary old chief named Pontiac was thinking the
matter over. "We cannot drive the English into the
ocean," he thought, "but if all our tribes should unite

and help the French, then the Frenchmen might rule in Canada again, and they would help us against all our enemies." He sent messengers to many tribes to say: "The English hate us. They want to kill us, or drive us far away from the hunting grounds that the Great Spirit gave to our fathers. Will you join with us to thrust these enemies of ours from the land? The French say that their king has been asleep, but that he will soon awake and send soldiers as many as the stars of the heavens."

Far and near the Indians replied, "We have heard your message; we have danced the war-dance; we are ready to fight." This dance was performed at night. The warriors put on their war-feathers and painted their faces with the colors that meant war. They seated themselves on the ground in a circle around a painted post, the firelight flashing on their beads and other ornaments. Behind them was the dark and gloomy forest. Soon the war-chief, the one chosen to lead them to the fight, sprang forward and dashed into the ring. He recited the deeds of the heroes of the tribe, how many enemies they had slain, how many scalps they had brought home. He rushed at the post and struck it fiercely with his hatchet as if it were his foe. He drew his scalping knife and pretended to be taking a scalp. He howled and shouted and yelled. The other warriors sprang from their places and leaped into the ring. They danced wildly about, brandishing knives and clubs and hatchets and tomahawks. They whooped and screeched until the whole forest echoed with the horrible clamor. Then they were ready to go on the warpath.

Pontiac planned that several of the principal forts or

INDIAN DANCE

settlements of the English should be attacked on the same day. Detroit was the strongest of these settle ments. " Detroit is mine," said Pontiac. " I know how to get into the fort." Now Pontiac's home was not far from Detroit. He and his braves went on the hunt in the winter; but when spring had come, they returned to their village. One fine spring day he went to the gate of the fort at Detroit with fifty of his men and said, " We wish to do honor to our friends, the English, and we are come to dance the calumet dance before you." The English did not like to admit so many Indians, but finally they replied, " You may come in." The braves who did not dance strolled about the fort as the Indian visitors usually did. They were noticing carefully just how the streets ran and where the houses were placed; but the English paid no special attention to what they were doing. After they had gone, the English said, " The Indians are friendly. There will be no trouble."

A little later a white woman saw the Indians filing off the muzzles of their guns. " They are planning some trickery," declared one of the settlers, and he warned Gladwyn, who commanded the fort. Another warning came from a young Indian girl. " Pontiac and his chiefs are coming here," she said. " They have made their guns short, and every brave will bring one hidden in his blanket. They will say they wish to hold a council with the whites, but when Pontiac gives the signal with a wampum belt, they will kill every Englishman in the fort."

Pontiac came as she had predicted, and asked for a council. The gates were flung open, and he and his braves walked in. Indians do not like to show their feelings, but Pontiac was so taken by surprise that he could

UNVEILING OF CONSPIRACY OF PONTIAC, DETROIT, 1763
From a Painting by J. M. Stanley

not keep back a grunt of disappointment. "They have found it out," he thought; and well he might think so, for all the soldiers of the place, fully armed, were drawn up in line on either side of the entrance. The fort was really a little village of about one hundred houses, and the council house was at the farther side. The Indians passed through the narrow streets and entered its doors. There sat Gladwyn and some of his officers, every one with sword and pistols.

" Why do my father's young men meet a friend with their guns? " asked the chief.

"The young men need exercise and drill," replied Gladwyn.

Pontiac hesitated, but at last he began to make a speech. He told the English how much he loved them and what a true friend he was. " I am come to smoke the peace-pipe with you," he said. The wampum belt was in his hands. He began to raise it as if to give a signal to his warriors; but Gladwyn also had a signal. He moved his hand, and in a moment they were deafened by the rolling of drums, the clash of arms, and the tramp of feet just outside the door. Then all was silence again. Gladwyn made his speech.

" We are your friends," he said, " and we have smoked the peace-pipe with you. But we are strong. We have many guns and many cannon. Our cannon speak with a loud voice, and they say, ' If the Indians are true, be good to them; but if they are not true, kill them and burn their villages.' "

" We are always the friends of the English," replied Pontiac. " We shall soon come again and bring with us our squaws and our children, that they may shake the hands of our fathers, the English."

" That speech is worth nothing," said Gladwyn to himself, and he set about strengthening the palisades and drilling his men. Early one morning, the attack which he expected was made. The air was filled with yells and shrieks. Bullets flew in showers. Hundreds of Indians were near the fort, but few could be seen, for they were hiding behind the crest of a hill. The soldiers returned their fire with a will, and they were driven away.

Gladwyn hoped that this was the end of the attack, but the trouble had only begun. Soon the Indians came again, and this time they came to stay. They made their camp a mile and a half away. Night and day they kept up their attack on the fort. Most of the little houses in the fort were thatched with straw, and the English did not dare to leave them a moment unguarded, for the Indians were shooting arrows to which burning rags were tied. Month after month the siege went on. The defenders were worn and weary. " Oh, if the English vessels would only come ! " they said.

At last the vessels came. They could see the English flag, and they shouted for joy. But the answer was the yell of savages. The Indians had seized the boats and slain the white men.

It was the beginning of May when the siege began. Week after week had passed, and October had come. To besiege a fort so long was new to the Indians, and many of them went away. Others took their places, but provisions were scarce and their powder nearly gone. Then one of the chiefs came to the fort.

"We are sorry for what we have done," he said,
"and we have brought the pipe of peace to smoke with
you. We have always been your friends."

"I did not begin this fight," replied Gladwyn.
"When my king tells me to stop, I will stop, and not
till then; but I am willing to have a truce."

In reality, Gladwyn was more than willing, for he,
too, was short of provisions. While the truce lasted, he
got in as much food as possible. It was all needed, for it
was more than fifteen months from the beginning of the
siege to its end. In the sixteenth month, the imprisoned
soldiers once more saw the red flag of England on the
river. They hardly dared to cheer for fear of being
deceived again, but now all was well. The boats were
English vessels with English troops on board. Cheer
after cheer rose from the fort, and never was the sound
of a cannon more welcome than that which they heard
in reply. The siege of Detroit was raised. Some of the
Indians fled, some begged for pardon. A little later a
council of whites and Indians was held. Here Pontiac
said, "I declare, in the presence of all the nations, that I
have made peace and taken the king of England for my
father."

The English never trusted Pontiac, and whenever
they heard that he was among the French they were
afraid of an attack. At length, an English fur trader
whispered to one of the Illinois Indians, "Do you want

a barrel of rum? Go into those woods and kill Pontiac, and it is yours." This was done, but fearful revenge followed the deed, for Pontiac's followers attacked the Illinois and destroyed almost their whole tribe. A French officer who had long been a friend of the dead warrior sent for his body and buried it with warlike honors.

OUTLINE

How the Algonquins felt at the capture of Quebec — Pontiac's plan — the war-dance — Pontiac visits Detroit — warnings given to the whites — Pontiac's council — Gladwyn prepares for an attack — Pontiac besieges the fort — the English vessels come in sight — Indians on board — Gladwyn grants a truce — English vessels come a second time — Pontiac's surrender — murder of Pontiac — revenge of his friends.

SUGGESTIONS FOR WRITTEN WORK

The Indians tell stories of the kindness of the French.
One of Pontiac's men describes the council at Detroit.
An Englishman at Detroit tells his friends about the siege.

THE FIRST DAY OF THE REVOLUTION

WHEN Braddock crossed the ocean to help fight the French and Indians, the colonists were glad to see the red coats of the British soldiers; but a few years later they were angry and indignant at having soldiers from England on American soil. The king had sent the troops to Boston because the colonists had refused to obey some unjust laws that he had made. He thought they would not dare to resist if the British regulars were among them.

The colonists were angry, but they were not frightened. " If we must fight, we will get ready," they said. In Miles Standish's time there had been companies of men that agreed to start for battle at half an hour's notice. Companies were now formed that said they would start at one minute's notice, and therefore they were called minute-men. The best soldiers cannot do much without ammunition. So the colonists began to store in Concord powder and shot, bombs and cartridge paper, spades and pickaxes, as well as beef, rice, salt fish, flour, and oatmeal.

Paul Revere, a goldsmith and engraver of Boston, was at the head of thirty men who made it their business to watch the British troops and the British man-of-war, the Somerset, anchored out in the harbor. One day they noticed that there was bustle and commotion among the redcoats on land, and that it was not as quiet as usual on board the Somerset. " Something is afoot," thought these wide-awake colonists. They kept their ears open as well as their eyes, and they caught a word or two that told them the whole story. " The British are going to Concord to destroy our stores," they said, " and to Lexington to capture our champions, Samuel Adams and John Hancock."

Some little time before this, General Gage had seized cannon and stores belonging to the colonists, and they did not mean to be caught napping a second time; so

THE RIDE OF PAUL REVERE

they decided to send William Dawes by way of Roxbury and Paul Revere by way of Charlestown to warn Adams and Hancock and the farmers who lived on the way. They could not find out whether the troops were to march from Boston by the Roxbury road or the Charlestown road. If by Roxbury, they would leave Boston by land; if by Charlestown, they would leave by water. Revere arranged a signal. "Hang a lantern in the tower of the North Church if they go by land," he said; "and hang two if they go by water." Then he rowed over to Charlestown. On the shore he waited and waited. It was nine o'clock, ten, eleven, and then a faint light gleamed in the tower. In a moment there was a second light. The British had started by water.

Then he sprang upon his horse and galloped toward Medford. "Halt!" cried a sharp voice, and there stood two British soldiers on guard, for Gage had given orders that no colonists should be allowed to leave Boston that night. "Dismount!" they commanded. But Revere dashed on. He roused every little village on the way and every farmhouse. "The regulars are coming!" he cried. "Get up and arm!"

The regulars were coming. They had been rowed across the Charles River and were marching on to Lexington. "Those stupid farmers will be surprised for once," they said to one another. "We'll wake them up." But over the fields they began to see lights in the windows of the farmhouses. They could hear in the darkness the village bells clanging out an alarm. Now and then a gun was fired. "The rebels have found it out!" they muttered. "Perhaps they do not know in

Lexington yet," thought the commander, and he hurried his men onward. But on Lexington Green were sixty or seventy minute-men, their guns in their hands.

MINUTE-MEN HURRYING TO CONCORD BRIDGE

"Disperse, you villains! You rebels, disperse!" shouted the British officer. The minute-men stood looking straight at the soldiers. "Fire!" shouted the officer, and the soldiers fired. Eight colonists were killed and ten were wounded. The minute-men returned the fire and wounded two soldiers. Another company of red-coats was coming up the road, and the colonists retreated. "Hurrah!" cried the soldiers. "Hurrah! Hurrah!"

Hancock and Adams had been warned and had left the place. There was no hope of getting them, but the stores could be destroyed at any rate, thought the British. So they marched on to Concord. They found the place where the stores had been, but they had disappeared, — the Concord men could have told where. The troops relieved their minds by setting the court-house afire and knocking in the heads of a few barrels of flour. Then came the minute-men, four hundred of them. They met two hundred British at the North Bridge. Both sides fired, then the colonists charged and the British retreated.

It was nearly ten o'clock in the morning. The British soldiers had been up all night. They had marched eighteen miles. They were tired and hungry. The commander stayed in Concord two hours to give them a chance to rest. He did not know how much the colonists could do in two hours, but he soon found out; for all this time the minute-men had been gathering from near and far. If they had marched out in rank and file and stood still to be shot at, the British would have

THE FIGHT AT CONCORD BRIDGE
From the painting by Edward Simmons in the State House at Boston

won the day; but these farmers had learned a good deal from their wars with the Indians. Every man hid behind a barn or a wall or a rock or a tree and fired. The British were as dazed as Braddock's men had been. They ran for their lives. They threw away their guns. They did not stop even to pick up the wounded.

News of what had been done had reached the British in Boston, and twelve hundred of them with two cannon came out to Lexington. They formed a hollow square, and into this the soldiers rushed and flung themselves on the grass, completely exhausted. They were on open ground, and the cannon soon drove the minute-men away. Indeed, they were not at all anxious to stay. The British would have to start again before long and march into Boston; they would do their fighting then — and they did. More and more minute-men came from all directions. They fired at the British from behind, from both sides, and even from ahead. At first the British stopped sometimes, swung their cannon around and returned the fire; but it was not so easy to know where to aim when the enemy seemed to be everywhere and nowhere at the same time. The British went fast and faster; they broke into a wild run. If they could only get to Charlestown, they thought, the guns of the Somerset would defend them. At last they reached Charlestown, but two hundred and forty-seven of their men had been killed and wounded. The colonists had lost eighty-eight. All this took place April 19, 1775, and that date marks the beginning of the Revolutionary War.

OUTLINE

British troops in Boston — minute-men — preparations for defense — a commotion among the British — the Americans plan to warn the farmers — Paul Revere's ride — the regulars march to Lexington — the meeting on Lexington Green — the march to Concord — the Concord fight — a two-hours' rest — the regulars return to Lexington — the march back to Boston.

SUGGESTIONS FOR WRITTEN WORK

The colonists plan to form companies of minute-men.

The talk of the regulars on the way to Lexington.

How the Concord men hid the stores.

A British soldier begins a letter, "On the night of the eighteenth of April:" Finish the letter.

ISRAEL PUTNAM

SOLDIER OF THE REVOLUTION

THERE was once a boy who made two visits to Boston, on each of which he got into a fight. The first time was when he was a little fellow, and a boy much larger than he kept calling after him, " Country, country ! " Thereupon he gave the saucy Boston boy a hard whipping, and went home to Salem. After some years he married, bought himself a piece of land on top of a Connecticut hill, and became a farmer. He was as fond

of his farm as if it had been one of his children, and was
especially proud of his fine breed of sheep. One morning he found that sixty or seventy of them had been
killed by a wolf. He and his neighbors joined in a
wolf - hunt and soon
had the beast shut
into its cave. Put-
nam lighted a torch,
went boldly into the
cave, shot the crea-
ture before it could
spring at him, and
came out dragging it.

When the French
and Indian War broke
out, he was ready to
fight. In one battle
his blanket was shot
through fourteen
times, but he was not
touched. Once the
barracks of a fort caught fire. Hundreds of barrels
of powder stood near them. Neither the commander
nor any one else seemed to have any idea what to do.
Putnam was not there, but he saw the smoke, ran to the
fort, and began to give orders. " Form in line ! " he
cried. " Pass the buckets along ! " He took his stand

ISRAEL PUTNAM

between the powder and the fire, and threw on the buckets of water as fast as they could be passed to him. The smoke and the whirl of the ashes in the wind almost hid him from the soldiers. The fire blazed around him. His heavy mittens were burned off his hands. "Take these!" cried some one, and gave him a pair soaked with water. The fire came nearer and nearer to the powder. One partition fell, another and another. Only a thin board wall stood between him and an awful explosion. Still he did not run, and at last he conquered. The flames died down, and he pulled off his wet mittens. The skin came with them, and then for the first time he discovered that he had been terribly burned.

Even that experience was less dreadful than a day that he spent with the Indians. His gun missed fire, and he was captured. They tied him to a tree and piled wood around him. It was kindled, and the flames blazed up. Then the Indians sang and danced and howled with delight. A few minutes more would have ended his life, but just then a French officer appeared on the scene. He rushed through the yelling crowd, kicked the fire to pieces, and cut the bonds.

During this same war, Putnam was on the St. Lawrence with General Amherst when he heard the general say, "We could soon capture the fort if it were not for the schooner over there that protects it."

"I'll take the schooner for you," Putnam offered, "if

you 'll give me some wedges and a mallet, and let me choose half a dozen men."

The general was beginning to find out that the Americans had their own way of doing things, and at length he actually gave Putnam permission to try his plan. When night came, the men got into a light boat, muffled their oars, and in the darkness rowed up to the stern of the schooner. They drove wedges between the rudder and the stern-post. Then they rowed in the shadow around to the bow and cut the anchor loose. The French soon found that they were adrift; but the rudder would not move, they were helpless, and they floated ashore with nothing to do but surrender. The fort followed their example.

At the close of the war, in 1764, Putnam went home, hung up his sword, swung over his door a signboard with General Wolfe's picture on it, and for ten years was a quiet farmer and innkeeper. On the 20th of April, in 1775, he had eaten his dinner and gone out to the field with his oxen. Suddenly he heard the sound of a drum. A man was galloping furiously along the road, beating his drum and calling, " To arms ! To arms ! The British have fired upon us ! The country is ablaze!" Then Putnam forgot his beloved farm. He forgot to say good-by to his family. He forgot that he was an officer, and was going to war without his uniform. He forgot everything except which of his horses was the

THE BATTLE OF BUNKER HILL

swiftest. He leaped upon its back, and while the oxen stood in the field waiting patiently for him to return, he was galloping along the road to make his second visit to Boston, one hundred miles away.

The Continental Army had gathered from all directions. The British were in possession of Boston. "We must seize those hills," declared the British General Gage, "if we are to stay in the city."

"We must seize those hills," declared the Americans, "if we are to drive the British out of the city." Colonel Prescott and General Putnam marched out by night and began to fortify Breed's Hill and Bunker Hill.

At daybreak the British discovered what was going on. "We might take Charlestown Neck," said one officer, "and starve them out."

"That's too slow," objected another. "I believe the best way will be to charge upon them."

"Not so easy to charge up that hill."

"Why not? They're only farmers. They don't know anything about fighting. The chances are that they will run long before we are at the foot of the hill."

So the British talked, and at length they decided to make a charge. The march began. The scarlet lines came nearer and nearer. Prescott and Putnam were going back and forth among their men at the top of the hill. "Remember there isn't much powder," they said. And Putnam added, "Men, you know how to aim. Don't fire till you can see the whites of their eyes."

Up the hill marched the British, stopping only to fire; but the Americans stood motionless. It seemed to them hours before the word rang out, "Fire!" That fire was like a cannonade, and the British, brave old

soldiers as they were, ran pell-mell down the hill.
" Hurrah! hurrah!" shouted the Americans. The British formed and rushed up the hill again; again the lines
broke, and they retreated. They came a third time, but
now no volleys met them; the powder had given out.
The Americans had no bayonets, but they fought furiously with stones and the butt ends of their muskets,
with clubs, knives, even with their fists; but no such
weapons could withstand British veterans, and the Americans had to retreat.

News of the battle went through the colonies like
wildfire. All their lives the Americans had looked up
to the British regulars as the greatest of soldiers: and
they, the untrained colonists who had never seen two
regiments in battle, had twice driven them back! The
hill was lost, but to repulse the British regulars was
a mighty victory. Couriers galloped from one colony
to another to carry the news. Everywhere there was
rejoicing; but Putnam could not bear to think that
after such a fight the hill had at last been given up,
and he growled indignantly, " We ought to have stood.
Powder or no powder, we ought to have stood."

OUTLINE

Putnam's first visit to Boston — his life on a farm — the wolf
hunt — in the French and Indian War — how he put out a fire
— Putnam among the Indians — he captures a schooner — he
becomes an innkeeper — what happened on April 20, 1775 —

British and Americans both determine to seize the hills overlooking Boston — British scorn of the colonists — the battle of Bunker Hill — feelings of the Americans.

SUGGESTIONS FOR WRITTEN WORK

A soldier describes Putnam's putting out of the fire.
Putnam's ride to Boston.
Putnam tells his family about the battle of Bunker Hill.

A CHRISTMAS SURPRISE

IT was Christmas night in 1776, the second year of the Revolutionary War, and the Hessian soldiers were making merry at Trenton. They were Germans who had been hired by the king of England to help him conquer the American rebels. Just then there was no fighting on hand. They had good warm quarters, plenty to eat, and plenty to drink. They feasted and they drank, they sang songs, and they told stories. They were in the best of spirits, for Washington, the commander-in-chief of the Americans, was retreating. "There won't be much more trouble from him," declared one soldier. "He had to leave the Hudson, and we have chased him out of New Jersey and into Pennsylvania."

"We'll soon be in Pennsylvania ourselves, in Philadelphia," said another, "and that will be the end of the

WASHINGTON AT THE DELAWARE

war. They say Washington's troops are deserting by the hundred."

The carousing went on until late in the night, and then the men went to their warm beds and to heavy sleep.

About the time that their feasting began, Washington marched his men down to the opposite bank of the Delaware. The ground was covered with snow. It was bitterly cold. The sleet was driving furiously. The river was full of masses of floating ice, pitching, tumbling, and plunging in the strong current; but boats were waiting at the shore. They were rowed by fishermen from Marblehead who knew how to meet storms. The soldiers got into the boats. The fishermen rowed and paddled, and pushed away the cakes of ice with long poles. The wind blew more furiously, the sleet was more biting; but at last the boats came to the New Jersey side of the river. The men leaped or tumbled ashore as well as they could in the storm and darkness. Then they swung their arms, they stamped their feet, they marched back and forth, they jumped, and they ran — anything to keep from freezing. The storm was growing worse; there was no shelter; and on the river bank they must wait till the boats had been back and forth many times and had brought the whole force across. Ten hours they waited, all through that terrible night of tempest.

Trenton was nine miles away, but Washington had given the word to march on. One man was frozen to death, and a little later a second was overcome by the cold. "The muskets are wet and cannot be fired," an officer reported.

"Use the bayonets, then," replied Washington; "the town must be taken." And he pushed on toward Trenton. He divided his men into two parties, and in the early gray of the morning they entered the town by two different roads.

Washington planted his cannon so as to sweep the streets. The Hessians rushed out, almost dazed by the sudden attack. They ran in one direction, and a volley of musket balls met them; they ran in another, and the cannon mowed them down; in another, and a bayonet charge drove them back. The commander ran out half-dressed and tried to form his lines, but he was shot down. In one hour Washington was master of the place. He had lost two men, and he had taken nearly one thousand prisoners.

The British general, Cornwallis, was in New York, getting ready to return to England; for he thought the rebellion of the colonies was so nearly over that he need not stay in America any longer. The news from Trenton was an unpleasant surprise, but he started out promptly to crush that troublesome Washington, who never seemed to understand

A HESSIAN GRENADIER

that he was beaten and who would not stay beaten.

Cornwallis had more men than the Americans, and

Washington did not want to fight a battle with him.
" Cornwallis will come upon us, but keep him away as
long as you can," was Washington's order to part of his
troops; and therefore the British had a hard time in
their march across New Jersey to Trenton. A storm of
bullets would come suddenly from some little thicket
on one side of the road; and by the time the trees had
been well peppered with British shot, another leaden
storm would come from some thicket on the other side.
A few hundred men with two cannon were continually
attacking him in front. He could make them retreat,
but he could not make them hurry; and it was late in
the afternoon when he came to Trenton. Washington
was not in the town, but just across a stream that flows
into the Delaware. The troops that had been such a
torment to Cornwallis retreated across the bridge and
joined their comrades.

The British officers said, "Let us attack him at once."
But Cornwallis replied, "No, our men are tired out, and
it will soon be dark. He is safe enough. In the morning
we shall have two thousand more troops, and we can
shut him in between the stream and the Delaware. He
will have to surrender, and then the rebellion will be
over." He wrote a letter home which said, " We have
run down the old fox, and we will bag him in the
morning."

There seemed nothing that Washington could do but

prepare to fight. All night long his camp-fires burned along the south side of the stream. The British sentinels on the north side could see the men piling on wood, they could hear the noise of spades and pickaxes, they

THE SURRENDER OF COLONEL RALL AT THE BATTLE OF TRENTON

could even hear the soldiers talking together. But when it began to grow light, the British found that Washington and his army had slipped away quietly in the middle of the night. A few men had remained behind to keep the fires burning and make as much noise as possible with their spades and pickaxes; but they, too, were gone. They had run through the woods and joined their commander. The British were welcome to the gravel that had been shoveled up and to the ashes of the camp-fires, but nothing else was left for them. While Cornwallis stood on the bank of the stream gazing across at the deserted camp, he heard the booming of cannon ten miles away. " That was from Princeton," he thought. " The old fox is there already, and he will try to destroy our stores at Brunswick."

This was exactly what Washington had planned to do. At Princeton he met the British forces just starting to go and help Cornwallis conquer him. There was a sharp fight, and the Americans won the day. Cornwallis was in pursuit, of course, but there were several streams between the armies. They were badly swollen by a sudden thaw, and Washington had unkindly burned the bridges. The British marched with dripping uniforms into the streets of Princeton, but Washington was not there. He had hoped to go on to Brunswick, but his men were too tired and too nearly barefooted for a march of eighteen miles. So he made his way to the heights of Morristown, and there he was safe for the winter.

OUTLINE

The Hessians at Trenton — the Christmas celebration — the soldiers talk of Washington — Washington crosses the Delaware — the storm — waiting on the shore — the march to Trenton — the capture of Trenton — Cornwallis pursues Washington to the

Delaware — Cornwallis postpones his attack — Washington slips away — the battle of Princeton — Washington goes to Morristown.

SUGGESTIONS FOR WRITTEN WORK

One of Washington's soldiers describes the crossing of the Delaware.

A Hessian soldier tells the story of Christmas night.

The letter that Cornwallis wrote home on Christmas Eve, and the postscript that he added the day after Christmas.

A WINTER AT VALLEY FORGE

DURING the Revolution the British had the idea that it would be a great thing if they could take Philadelphia. They called it " the rebel capital," because Congress had met there; and they did not seem to realize that Congress could easily meet somewhere else. They marched into the city with colors flying and bands playing, and Washington could not prevent them. When they were once in, the best thing for him to do was to see that they did not get out to do any mischief; and so he chose for his winter quarters Valley Forge, a place only a few miles from Philadelphia. There he could easily defend himself if he was attacked, and he could keep close watch of the British.

It would have been easier to fight many battles than to spend that winter in Valley Forge. It was December, and there was no shelter of any kind. Men and officers set to work bravely to build huts for themselves. These huts were of all sorts. Some were built of heavy logs. Their roofs were made of small trees wrapped with straw and laid side by side. Clay was spread on top of the straw, and splints were laid on top of that. The windows were simply holes cut through the logs and covered with oiled paper.

A house like this was looked upon as the height of luxury. Most of the huts were made of sods piled up,

WASHINGTON'S HEADQUARTERS AT VALLEY FORGE

or fence rails or poles held together by twigs twisted in and out and daubed with clay. The snow sifted in at every little opening, the rain dripped through even the best of the roofs, and the wind howled and roared and blew in at every crevice. There were few blankets, and many brave defenders of their country lay on the frozen ground because they had not even straw to put under them. Sometimes they sat up all night, crowding up to the fires to keep from freezing.

They were no better off for clothing than for houses. The whole army was in rags, which the soldiers' most skillful mending could hardly hold together. Many of the men had no shirts, even more were without shoes. Wherever they walked, the snow was marked with blood. Some cut strips from their precious blankets, and wound them about their feet to protect them from the frozen ground. Food was scanty; sometimes for several days they were without meat, and some companies were once without bread for three days. When the word went around, "No meat to-night," the soldiers groaned, but they never yielded.

The cause of these hardships was the fact that Congress had no power. It could say to a state, "We need money for the army, and your share will be so much;" but if the state did not choose to pay the tax, Congress could not force it to pay. It is said that while these brave soldiers were suffering in their rags, whole hogsheads of clothes and shoes and stockings were waiting at different places on the roads until money to pay for teaming could be found. Sometimes the soldiers themselves took the places of horses and oxen, and when they could learn of any supplies, dragged the wagons into camp.

Washington shared all this suffering with his men, and he had even more to bear from fault-finders. The Pennsylvania legislature thought he ought not to shelter his men in huts at Valley Forge. "Why doesn't he camp out in tents in the open field," they demanded, "and attack the British?" This was too much for even Washington's patience, and he wrote a blunt letter to the legislature, telling them how little they were doing for the army. He said it was much easier to find fault " in a comfortable room by a good fireside than to camp upon a cold, bleak hill and sleep under frost and snow without clothes or blankets."

Not all the soldiers were Americans by any means. Some of them were foreigners who had come to America to get what they could out of the country ; but there were also many who came because they believed that the United States was in the right, and they wanted to help her win her independence. One of these true friends was a young Frenchman, the Marquis de Lafayette. For some time the Americans had been trying to persuade France to help them, but Lafayette could not bear to wait for his country to act. "The moment I heard of America, I loved her," he wrote. He fitted out a ship at his own cost and crossed the ocean. Then he asked two "favors" of Congress, — to serve as a volunteer, and to pay his own expenses. Congress made him an officer, although he was only nineteen. He won the heart of the commander-in-chief at their first meeting, and from that day Washington trusted him as he trusted few people.

WASHINGTON AND LAFAYETTE AT VALLEY FORGE

Lafayette was rich, a nobleman, and a favorite at the French court. He had lived in luxury all his days; but he shared with Washington the hard life at Valley Forge, never complaining, always bright and cheerful. All this time he was writing letters home, which did much to bring about something that delighted Washing-

ton and "the boy," as the British scornfully called Lafayette. Word came across the sea that the French
king had decided to help America. Then there was
rejoicing at gloomy Valley Forge. A day of thanks-
giving was appointed. Prayer was offered, the troops
were reviewed, thirteen cannon were fired, and at a
signal the whole army shouted, "Long live the king
of France!"

The French government had asked many questions
about the American army. The answer was always the
same, "They are brave and patient and determined, but
they lack drill and discipline. They are splendid fighters, but they need to be taught how to fight together."
There was a Prussian officer, Baron von Steuben, who
was better prepared than any one else to teach what the
army ought to know, and the French persuaded him to
cross the ocean.

The baron was amazed when he went to Valley
Forge and saw the miserable little huts and the starving, half-naked men. "There is not a commander in
Europe who could keep troops together a week if they
were suffering like this," he declared. There was
hardly any artillery and almost no cavalry. Many of
the guns were not fit to use. Few of them had bayonets. That was a small matter, however, for the
soldiers did not know what to do with bayonets, and
had used them chiefly to broil meat with — when they

were so fortunate as to have any meat. Baron von Steuben was horrified. He drilled and drilled. One minute he stormed at the ignorance of the men, and

BARON VON STEUBEN

the next he praised their quickness in learning some difficult movement. Then at their next blunder he stormed again in a comical mixture of German and

French and English. In spite of his scoldings, however, he was devoted to the men and exceedingly proud of them. During that cruel winter many fell ill, and the hot-tempered baron went about from one wretched hut to another, doing everything that he could to help and cheer them. It is no wonder that they loved him and were eager to learn.

The terrible winter at Valley Forge came to an end at last. Out of the cold and hunger and sickness and suffering an army came forth that was stronger than before, an army that was " never beaten in a fair fight."

OUTLINE

The British march into Philadelphia, and Washington encamps at Valley Forge — the huts at Valley Forge — the need of blankets, clothes, and food — the cause of these hardships — grumbling of the fault-finders —Washington's reply — foreign soldiers — Lafayette — France promises help — the rejoicing at Valley Forge — character of the American army — the coming of Von Steuben — the condition of the soldiers — Von Steuben drills them — his kindness to them.

SUGGESTIONS FOR WRITTEN WORK

A soldier tells his children of his hut at Valley Forge ; of Lafayette : of Von Steuben.

HOW "MAD ANTHONY" TOOK STONY POINT

IN the Revolutionary War the British were especially anxious to get possession of the Hudson River. If they could only hold that, they could separate the American army into two parts, one in New England and one in the Middle and Southern States. Neither part could get out of its corner, and the British could conquer first one and then the other. In their first attempt to capture the Hudson they failed. Nearly two years later they seized a fort on the river at Stony Point. Then they began to send parties of soldiers to burn towns and kill Americans in Connecticut.

Washington thought, "The British want me to send my men to protect the people of Connecticut, and when my soldiers are fighting there, they will take more forts on the Hudson. I will not send my men away, but I will storm the fort at Stony Point, and then the British will have to leave Connecticut to help the army in New York."

Stony Point was "little but mighty." It was on a high point of land that ran out into the Hudson, and it was cut off from firm land by a swamp. Across the swamp ran a raised walk, but even this was over-flowed by the tide twice a day. The Americans had begun this fort; then the British had captured it and done everything they could to make it strong. They had piled entirely around it two rows of logs, rocks, briers, earth, or whatever else would be hard to cross. Farther up the hill were fortifications fairly bristling with cannon. More than six hundred British were guarding the place. Such was the fort that Washington determined must be taken.

Who should be the leader? The fort must be captured by a sudden dash; a man was needed who was not afraid of guns or soldiers, and he must be cool enough to think while balls were flying and bombs were exploding around him. "Anthony Wayne is the one," thought Washington. "He does not know what it means to be afraid, and he always has his wits about him. He'll storm anything on earth. If Stony Point can be taken, he will take it."

Soldiers always nickname their favorite generals, and General Wayne they called "Mad Anthony" because he was so daring. They were ready to follow him anywhere. When the night came that Washington had set, Wayne and his troops marched in Indian file silently up the bank of the Hudson. They came near enough to the black fort to hear the sentinel call, "Twelve o'clock! All's well!" They crept on softly. It was high tide, and the swamp was a pond; but they marched straight in. Then the alarm was given. There was a

clash of arms, a firing of muskets, a terrific blaze of
cannon; but the Americans pressed on as if the tempest
of grapeshot were only a summer shower. Every man
knew his place and his work. They formed in two columns, each headed by twenty men with axes, whose
business it was to clear a way through the logs and rub-
bish. They were mowed down by the grapeshot, but their
work was done, and the two columns rushed in through
the two gaps that
they had made. In
the cap of every
man was a bit of
white paper, so that
in the darkness he
would not be mis-
taken for an ene-
my. Not a gun was
loaded. Such forts
as Stony Point are
not taken by mus-
ket-balls. One col-
umn tore up the
hill from the right;
General Wayne

ANTHONY WAYNE

headed the other from the left. He was struck by a
ball and fell. But his voice rang out in the horrible
tumult, " Carry me into the fort, for I will die at the

head of my column! March on!" They caught him up and dashed forward.

Nothing could drive them back. They swarmed over the ramparts. They fought their way with better weapons than powder and shot. They were like a moving wall of bristling steel, for Baron von Steuben had taught them how to use bayonets. The attack was so sudden, so well planned, so irresistible that nothing could turn them. In a few minutes Wayne's column was in the centre of the fort, and in front of them was the other line that had come up the other side of the hill. There was no silence then, but wild shouts, "Hurrah! hurrah! hurrah!" The fort was theirs, and the British garrison were their prisoners. Cannon, muskets, balls, powder, provisions were all in their hands. The general's wound was not so serious as he had thought, and he lived to do much more brave fighting for his country.

The capture of the British stronghold without the firing of a gun was talked over in every camp. Baron von Steuben cried, "That is good, that is good. Now we are beginning to walk!" From Philadelphia came a letter to Wayne which said, "You will be stunned with your own praises. Our streets for many days rang with nothing but the name of General Wayne. You are remembered constantly next to our good and great Washington!"

THE STORMING OF STONY POINT

" "Carry me into the fort, for I will die at the head of my column !"

One story that shows how quickly Wayne could see
what was the best move to make ought to be told here.
He was in Virginia just before the end of the war.
"The British have crossed the river. Only a small rear-

guard are left on this side. Attack them!" This was the order given to him. He marched straight toward the British lines; but some one had made a mistake; before him was no rear-guard, but the whole force of the British army, and he had only seven hundred men! The enemy was already coming toward him. There were two or three things that he could do. He could surrender; but he objected to surrenders. He could retreat; but the British were in line ready to pursue, and he would be captured before he could fairly get to running. He could charge upon the great army and go down in history as a man who would rather die than yield; but he preferred to stay alive and strike a few more blows at the British. In a moment he had decided. "Charge!" he commanded, and the little band dashed forward so fearlessly that Cornwallis, the British commander, supposed a large force was behind them and began to bring his men together to repulse a general attack. Five minutes more, and he would have learned his mistake; but Wayne did not give him the five minutes. The instant that Cornwallis had set his men in motion, Wayne cried, "About face!" And before the enemy had discovered what had happened, he was retreating in safety.

There are many such stories as these of "Mad Anthony," the man who would dash upon the enemy like a tornado, and be as clear-headed in the midst of a battle as in his own home.

OUTLINE

Why the British wished to hold the Hudson — their object in
sending men to Connecticut — Washington plans to take Stony
Point — situation of Stony Point — the choice of a leader — why
called " Mad Anthony " — the march to the fort — the attack —
Wayne is wounded — using the bayonets — capture of the fort —
praise of the soldiers — the story of Wayne's charging the British
army.

SUGGESTIONS FOR WRITTEN WORK

Washington tells his plan for storming Stony Point to " Mad
Anthony," and asks him if he will take the lead.

The march up the Hudson.

A British soldier who was at Stony Point describes the attack.

HOW THE " SWAMP FOX " MADE THE BRITISH MISERABLE

AFTER the British had been trying for four years
to conquer America and had not succeeded, they
concluded that it would be an excellent plan to begin
at the south and work toward the north. They did not
find this an easy thing to do, and they had an especially
hard time in South Carolina, all because of a slender,
dark, silent, courteous little gentleman named Francis
Marion.

Marion brought together a few men and proceeded to
make the enemy miserable. He had no money for uni-

forms, and his men wore whatever they could get. For arms, they carried anything that looked like a gun; and if they wanted swords, they took saws to the country blacksmith and had them hammered into weapons which were not very handsome, but which they knew how to make useful. For bullets they melted pewter dishes and ran the metal into moulds. When there was nothing better, they used buckshot or even swanshot. For rations they ate whatever they could get; Marion himself could live for weeks on hominy or rice or potatoes. They had no pay, no hope of promotion, hardly any blankets; but they had horses that could go like the wind, they had keen wits and muscles that were like steel, and they were devoted to their country.

FRANCIS MARION

These were the men who were such a torment to the British. No one ever knew where they were. No one could tell how to avoid them. When twilight came,

Marion gave the order and they started for somewhere, he alone knew where. Sometimes they waded through a swamp, sometimes crept through fields and valleys close to the camp of the enemy, sometimes galloped fearlessly along the open road, sometimes stealthily followed on the track of the hostile lines. If ever any company of soldiers straggled away from the main army, then let them look out for Marion and his men! There would be a sudden rush from some valley or thicket, the bullets would fly from all sides, and in five minutes those that had not been shot would find themselves prisoners. Wherever Marion's men went, some deed of daring always ended their journey. Once Marion actually galloped into a village where a company of the enemy were encamped and seized the commander. There were not always guns enough to go around. Then the men waited patiently or fought with their blacksmith swords till guns could be taken from the enemy. One night Marion's scouts reported, " Some British soldiers are coming down by the river to-morrow, and they will have with them one hundred and fifty American prisoners." " Forward march!" commanded Marion. He knew that the British would have to go through a narrow pass. He took possession of this, and when they came along early in the morning, his men attacked them both in front and behind so suddenly that they lost their heads completely. They fired once and then forgot their prisoners and ran for their lives, while the rescuers laughed to see them go.

Marion could look upon the British soldiers as men who were doing what they thought was their duty, but he had no patience with the Tories, as those Americans were called who stood by the king. If any Tories tried to hold a meeting, Marion was sure to find it out, and his bullets would go rattling among them. If he could hear of a Tory camp, his men would fall upon it like a whirlwind. Once after such a raid, one of his boldest riders chased the Tory commander at full gallop till both were far away from the rest of Marion's men. The other Tories, too, were fleeing for their lives; but suddenly they turned. This pursuer saw nothing but the man whom he was chasing until in a moment he found the whole Tory force coming upon him. He did not hesitate an instant, but waved his sword and shouted over his shoulder, " Come on, boys; here they are ! " and then charged. The Tories never dreamed that he was alone, and they ran away faster than ever, lest they should be captured by the terrible " Swamp Fox."

Marion's headquarters were on an island in the Pedee River. There the horses were always saddled, the men always ready. More volunteers flocked to this island, as daring, fearless, and devoted as his first followers. When they wished to go home, they went. No authority ever brought them back, but they always returned.

Marion was not always fortunate. His island encampment was utterly destroyed, and for once he was dis-

MARION ON A RAID

couraged. "Go to my men," he said. "Tell them I may
be forced to the mountains, and ask them if they will
stand by me till the British are driven from the land."

The answer came back, " Every man will stand by you till death." Then Marion was ready for anything. He set out to help General Lee capture a fort. At first matters looked almost hopeless. There stood the fort forty feet above them, safe and strong on a little mound. It would be the easiest thing in the world for the garrison to shoot any number of men trying to storm it. One of Marion's followers thought of a plan. At the word of command, they all disappeared into the forest. For five days and nights they chopped down trees, measured and cut and fitted the logs. Then came a night when they dragged them out and put them in place, and, behold, when the men in the fort gazed around in the morning, there stood a wooden tower, high enough to overlook their fort. A platform at the top was covered with men, all ready to fire at the word of command, and more of these sure marksmen were at the base. It is no wonder that the fort surrendered.

Marion and his men did not make these wild raids for the sake of adventure. It was partly to torment and weaken the enemy and partly to encourage the patriots. Some soldiers fought for gain, for honors, for promotion; but he and his followers fought for patriotism, for pure love of their country and devotion to freedom.

OUTLINE

The British plan to begin at the south and work toward the north — Marion's army — their expeditions — some of their attacks — Marion and the Tories — Marion's headquarters — his misfortune and appeal to his men — how he captured a fort — why Marion fought.

SUGGESTIONS FOR WRITTEN WORK

One of Marion's men tells how he got his arms and clothes; how the men rescued the prisoners at the pass; how the Tory commander was pursued.

GEORGE ROGERS CLARK

WHO GAVE THREE STATES TO THE UNION

ONE day during the Revolution a bill was brought before the English Parliament for supplies needed to carry on the war with the colonies. One item on this bill was for scalping-knives. " What does this mean ? " demanded a member. " Have our soldiers become savages? Are they scalping our colonists? " He was almost right. The English soldiers were not using scalping-knives, but Colonel Hamilton, governor of the country north of the Ohio, was giving them to the Indians to use in scalping Americans.

This land had been in the hands of the French until Canada was conquered. Then the British took possession of the forts. South of the Ohio there were many American colonists. They were bold, hardy people who had not been afraid to strike out into the wilderness and make homes for themselves far away from the cities and villages of the East. Hamilton hired the Indians to make attacks on these settlers. A colonist working in his field would be struck down by an Indian bullet; his wife and children would be fastened into their log cabin and burned to death. Some were taken prisoners, some were burned at the stake, some were horribly tortured. The settlers, men and women, held out bravely. Their guns were always loaded, they were always on their guard. " These are our homes," they said, " and we shall defend them."

One of these courageous settlers was a young surveyor named George Rogers Clark. He was a good fighter; he was also a good thinker. He thought a good deal about the Indian attacks, and then he said to two young hunters, " Will you go north of the Ohio and find out how the French settlers feel toward us?" When the hunters came back, they said, " Sometimes the French start out with the British and Indians and do a little fighting, but they don't really care a straw who wins. They are mightily afraid of us backwoodsmen, though."

Clark did not explain why he wanted to know about the people of the Ohio country. He said good-by and

set off over the mountains for Virginia. He had a long
talk with Patrick Henry, who was then governor. Governor Henry said, "It is a brilliant plan; but if it is
going to succeed, not
even the legislature
must know of it, for it
would be sure to leak
out."

"How much help can
you give me?" asked
Clark.

"We can give you a
little money," the gov-
ernor replied, "and we
can publish a notice
saying that you have
the right to raise men
to defend our colonists
south of the Ohio.

GEORGE ROGERS CLARK

From the portrait by Jarvis in possession
of the Wisconsin Historical Society

There is no need of
saying how you mean
to do it. We cannot do anything more without the vote
of the legislature."

For several months Clark worked to raise men, and
then he and his fighters went on board their flatboats at
Pittsburg. It was a thousand miles to the Mississippi,
but on the way they heard news that cheered their

courageous hearts. "The king of France has decided at last," were the tidings, "and he is going to help us. He will give us money and ships and men." No better news could have come to Clark than this. He called his men together and told them his plan. "We try to defend one settlement," he said, "and the savages come down upon another. The only way to stop it is to keep the British from sending the Indians."

"That's true enough," the men agreed, "but how do you propose to do that little thing?"

"I propose," replied Clark, "to go straight into the country north of the Ohio and capture their forts."

"Whew!" said the men.

Clark went on, "The French don't care whether we or the English win; but say to them, 'Your King Louis is on our side,' and they will prick up their ears. There'll be no trouble with the French."

The men became as enthusiastic as their leader, and set off on a march of fifty miles. They forded rivers, waded through swamps, tramped over prairies, forced their way through forests, and finally came in the darkness close to the settlement of Kaskaskia. Clark had about two hundred men. One hundred he ordered to surround the village; to the other hundred he said, "Follow me. Our work is to take the fort."

Clark had expected cannon balls, but there is a story that he was received with another kind of ball. As he

quietly approached the fort, he heard laughter and merriment; then music struck up and dancing began. He
slipped in through a little gate and stood in the doorway
a minute before any one noticed him. Some Indians
were in the room. One caught sight of him and gave a
warwhoop. The dancers stopped as if they were turned
to stone. The fiddler stood with his bow in the air and
his mouth wide open. "Go on with your dancing," said
Clark, "but understand that you are no longer subjects
of the king of Great Britain. This place is in the hands
of Virginia." This was true, for while Clark was con-
quering the ballroom, his men had captured the officers
of the fort.

Nobody thought of resisting. "Go to your houses,"
bade Clark. "The streets are in the hands of my men,
and they have orders to shoot any one who appears
outside his door." All night long the French hid away
in the darkness of their houses, dreading what might
come with the daylight. In the morning some of the
principal men of the little place asked to see Clark.
"Will you give us our lives?" they pleaded. "We
ask for nothing else, but do not put us to death."

Now Clark never dreamed of such a thing as putting
them to death, but he thought he could manage them
better if they had first been badly frightened. "I am
not here to kill any one," he replied. "The British have
made slaves of you, and I have come to set you free.

All I want is that you should swear to be true to the Americans. I can give you a piece of news. Your King Louis of France is our friend, and he is going to send us ships and money." Then the people of the frightened little village were wild with delight. Take the oath of allegiance? Of course they would. They were only too happy to take it. Vincennes and two or three other forts yielded. Many of the French joined Clark's lines and agreed to help fight the British.

When Hamilton heard of this, he dashed off with a strong force and took Vincennes. Then he stopped. " There is no use in making that hard march to Kaskaskia before spring," he thought. " One hundred men can garrison this place." So he sent most of his troops back to Detroit.

Unluckily for Hamilton, Clark was not afraid of a winter march, even one that was two hundred and forty miles long. Perhaps even he, however, did not guess what lay before him. He had a worse enemy to meet than bullets or cold or snow; and that was a February thaw. Floods came rolling down into the rivers, and every little stream became an angry torrent. The forest was deep in water, but the men clung to trees and bushes and floated on logs. A little " antic drummer," as Clark called him, floated over one river on his drum. The next stream was so deep that even these courageous men drew back. Clark lifted the little drummer to the shoulders of the giant of the company. The little fellow beat the charge. " Forward march ! " cried Clark, and the men plunged into the river in the best of spirits. Sometimes the water was frozen over, and they had not

THE LITTLE "ANTIC DRUMMER"

only to wade through water breast-high, but to break their way through the thin ice.

Hamilton saw their camp-fire one night, and sent out soldiers to find what it meant; but it did not occur to them to wade through a mile or two of deep water, and therefore they did not discover the Americans on what

Clark called " a delightful dry spot." Clark dashed up to the fort and began to fire. Hamilton defended himself as well as he could, but soon he had to send out a flag of truce and surrender.

Without these forts the British could not hold the Ohio country. American settlers poured into it; and when the Revolution was over and the time came to make a treaty of peace, the Americans said to England, " Your Canada comes as far south as the Great Lakes; but south of those the land is ours and is occupied by our settlers." Of this land, Ohio, Indiana, and Illinois were made; and therefore these three states are the gift of George Rogers Clark.

OUTLINE

A bill for scalping-knives — settlers in the Ohio country — attacks of the Indians — George Rogers Clark sends out spies — their report — Clark's talk with Patrick Henry — Clark's journey to Pittsburg — he hears good news — his plan — the march to Kaskaskia — Clark goes to a ball — an anxious night for the French — they go to see Clark — Hamilton takes Vincennes, but goes no farther — Clark meets a February thaw — how the drummer traveled — Hamilton surrenders — the Ohio country in American hands.

SUGGESTIONS FOR WRITTEN WORK

Clark tells his plan to Patrick Henry.
What Clark's men said of his plan.
The Kaskaskia fiddler tells of Clark's coming.
The drummer tells how he crossed the rivers.

JOHN PAUL JONES

AND HIS SEA FIGHTS FOR AMERICA

"THAT little boat will never get into harbor in such a squall," cried a ship-owner excitedly.

"He 'll fetch her in," declared a Scotchman who sat calmly watching the small craft in her struggle against the wind. "That 's my boy John in the boat. This is n't much of a squall for him."

The boat came in, and the ship-owner said, " John, I have a fine new vessel that is going to make a voyage to Virginia. If your father is willing, I will ship you as sailor." However the father may have felt, the boy was willing. He was only twelve, but for two years he had been begging to go to sea.

So he made the voyage to Virginia and also many other voyages. Before he was twenty he was a captain, and a well-known one, too. He lived in Virginia for a time, and while there he made up his mind that England and her colonies would be at war before many years had passed. On leaving Virginia, he said to George Washington, " Colonel, when the time comes that the colonies need me, I 'll be ready." The battle of Lexington took place only four months after he had made that speech, and he immediately sailed away in the service of the colonies. He captured a number of small English cruisers. One big frigate chased him, firing broadsides after him, and the captain probably became exceedingly angry, as Captain Jones saucily returned his broadsides with an occasional musket-shot. Two vessels that he took were full of supplies that had been meant for the British army; and there was joy in Boston when two whole shiploads of tents, blankets, saddles, ammunition, medicines, guns, cloaks, boots, and woolen shirts were landed.

PAUL JONES
From the portrait by Peale in
Independence Hall

This was all very well, but Captain Jones wanted to cross the ocean and show Britain on her own coast what the new States could do. In Portsmouth, New Hampshire, a ship named the Ranger had just been launched, and he was put in command. A few days earlier, Congress had decided that the flag of the United States should be "Thirteen Stripes, Alternate Red and White; that THE UNION be Thirteen Stars in a Blue Field." There was no flag for the Ranger; but the Portsmouth girls put their heads together and planned a "quilting party." They did not sew on calico patchwork, however, but on pieces of silk cut from their own best gowns. When they went home, they carried with them a beautiful silken flag; and this they presented to Captain Jones. He hurried down from Boston to fly the new banner on the Fourth of July, 1777, for the first time. Then he sailed away to see how many English banners he could lower.

His first cruise was around the north of Ireland. In the harbor of Carrickfergus was the British man-of-war, the Drake. "The wind is wrong, and I will wait a little," thought Jones. So he sailed past the harbor and waited. Three days later, some fishermen said, "The Drake is coming out in search of you."

"Good," cried Jones. "That will save me the trouble of going in after her."

The Drake came out and hailed the stranger with, "What ship is that?"

"The American Continental ship Ranger," was the reply. "Come on; we are waiting for you."

Then came a battle. A Narragansett Indian boy from Martha's Vineyard was one of the seamen, and a most excellent one. His account of the battle was, "I like to see the big gun shoot. I like to hear the big noise of much battle. It delights me to walk on the deck of the enemy's big boat when we have taken it. I think, by and by, we will take a much bigger boat than the

Drake." This was quite big enough, however, to startle all England. Never before in modern times had a regular British man-of-war been captured by a less powerful vessel. For two hundred years England had been mistress of the seas, and she did not like this new way of doing things.

England was still more angry before Captain Jones's work was over. He gave up the Ranger, though he held on to the silken flag that the Portsmouth girls had made; and soon he was put in command of a larger vessel, the Bon Homme Richard. Off he sailed for the British Isles. He went up the Irish coast and around Scotland, capturing a vessel now and then to keep his hand in. Off Flamborough Head he caught sight of a fleet of merchant vessels protected by the Serapis. The merchant vessels spread all sail and scudded away for their lives. Captain Pearson of the Serapis hailed the stranger with, "What ship is that?" There was no reply, but the Bon Homme Richard put herself in a good position for a fight. "That is probably Paul Jones," said Captain Pearson. "If so, there is work ahead."

There was "work ahead." For two hours the firing went on. Then there was a moment's quiet. "Have you struck your colors yet?" called Captain Pearson.

"I have n't yet begun to fight," Captain Jones replied. In the smoke and the darkness the two ships swung alongside. Captain Jones ordered them to be lashed together, and he himself ran to help tie the ropes. Then came a most awful hand-to-hand combat in the darkness. Guns burst, and a great heap of cannon cartridges caught fire and exploded. Wide gaps were torn out of the

FIGHT BETWEEN THE SERAPIS AND THE BON HOMME RICHARD
From a painting by Richard Paton

sides of both vessels. Worst of all, one of the French ships that should have assisted the Bon Homme Richard was stupidly firing straight at her. " The ship is sinking!" cried a gunner, "Quarter, quarter!" Captain Pearson heard this cry, and again called, " Have you struck?"

"No!" thundered Captain Jones.

The master-at-arms had also heard the gunner's cry and had set free the prisoners that they had captured. "Go to the pumps," the captain commanded them. "If you won't pump, the ship goes to the bottom and you go with her!"

At last the fighting stopped. One ship had yielded, but in the tumult and the darkness hardly any one knew which. It was the Serapis.

But the Bon Homme Richard was fast sinking. The water was six feet deep in her hold. Captain Jones left her and took possession of the Serapis. The Bon Homme Richard rolled from side to side. She lurched and pitched and plunged. At the last her taffrail rose in the air for an instant, and the little silken flag that had never been conquered waved for the last time in the morning breeze. "And even now it is still flying somewhere at the bottom of the North Sea," said Captain Jones, "over the battered wreck of the good old ship that sank, disdaining to strike it."

After the war closed, there was nothing more for Captain Jones to do in America, and he entered the service of Russia. His love for the country for which he had done so much never grew less; and just before he went to Russia, he wrote to friends in America, " I can never renounce the glorious title of a citizen of the United States." When he died, he was buried in Paris; but many years later his body was brought to America and laid near the Naval Academy at Annapolis. He was the real founder of the American navy, and therefore it is most fitting that he should lie where American boys

THE CAPTURE OF THE SERAPIS

are trained to become brave seamen and defenders of their country.

OUTLINE

"John" in a squall — he goes to sea — his promise to Washington — how he kept it — he plans a voyage to the British Isles — a flag for the Ranger — he meets the Drake — the Indian boy's account of the battle — England is startled — the Bon Homme Richard meets the Serapis — a terrible sea fight — the Bon Homme Richard is abandoned and sinks — Jones enters the service of Russia — his love for America — his burial place.

SUGGESTIONS FOR WRITTEN WORK

A Portsmouth girl tells the other girls of her plan to make a flag.

The letter that they wrote to Captain Jones.

His reply, promising to be with them July 4, 1777.

DANIEL BOONE

THE KENTUCKY PIONEER

NOT every American who was living at the time of the Revolution fought in the army. Some helped to raise money; some aroused the interest of the French in the struggling colonies; and some extended the power of the United States by pushing their way into what was then the "far West." Daniel Boone was one of these bold settlers. When he was a boy, he lived in the wilderness of North Carolina. His father's house was built of great logs, notched at the ends so that they fitted together firmly. The spaces between them were made tight with clay. The roof was of rough boards, hewn from logs. The floor was made by cutting logs open in the middle and laying them side by side with the level surface up. A fireplace was built of stones; and it was a large one, for there was plenty of wood to be had for the cutting. Mr. Boone made his table by boring four holes into the floor, driving in stakes, and putting split logs on top of them. It was not a very handsome table, but it never tipped

DANIEL BOONE

over. The bedstead was made by letting two poles into the wall a few feet from the corner. At the place where they crossed, a stake was driven into the floor to hold them up. Upon these poles other poles and pieces of bark were laid. On top was placed a thick cushion of dried grass, and the whole was covered with a fur robe.

As the boy grew up, other houses were built near this, and in one of them he found the young girl who became his wife. One day their home was visited by a hunter who had been far beyond the mountains to what is now Kentucky. He said it was a beautiful land, with mild climate, fertile soil, plenty of game and fruit, wide prairies, noble rivers, and fine old forests. The more the two men talked of this wonderful land, the more Boone wanted to see it, and at length he and five others set out on a journey of hundreds of miles through the wilderness and over the mountains. He learned the country thoroughly, and the more he saw of it the better he liked it.

A little later, the governor of Virginia made war upon the Indians of Kentucky, and in this war Boone was one of the leaders. The Indians finally agreed to give up Kentucky to the whites; but when they found that a road was being cut through from the east to their old hunting-grounds, they were not pleased. Boone was in charge of this road-making. He and his party were fired at and several were killed. They were only a little company of backwoodsmen far away in the wilderness, but they had no idea of yielding. " Now is the time to keep the country, — while we are in it," Boone declared; and he set to work at once to build a fort on the Kentucky River.

This fort, like many of those built in the forest in the

early days, was half fort and half village. First a clearing was made, and a rectangle marked out about twice as long as it was wide. Around the sides of this rectangle ten log houses were built. Between the houses, heavy timbers, ten or twelve feet high and sharpened at the top, were driven into the ground close together; and in this way a stout fence, or palisade, was made. Few of the Indians of that part of the country had guns, and their arrows could not go through either the log houses or the palisade. If they attempted to come near, they would have to cross the large clearing, where there were no trees to dodge behind to escape the white men's bullets. If they succeeded in getting across the clearing and tried to put up ladders against the palisade in order to climb over, they would find that the corner houses projected a little beyond the others, and that in these houses small port-holes had been left, from which the white men could shoot. Indians very rarely besieged a place for any length of time; but if the whites kept themselves well supplied with food, even a siege would fail, for one corner of the fort almost overhung the river, so they could be sure of plenty of water.

Boone's wife and children were in North Carolina, and they were as eager to come to him in the new land as he was to have them. As soon as it was known how strong a fort had been built, others were ready to journey to Boonesborough, as the new village was named.

So long as these settlers stayed in the fort, they were safe; but they soon found that whoever went beyond its walls was in danger of being shot down by an Indian arrow. After the Revolutionary War began, the British hired the savages to attack the Americans; and now the Indians were well supplied, not only with tomahawks but with guns and powder. Hundreds of pioneers left the fertile lands of Kentucky and hurried back to the east. Boone and his family remained, and he became the guardian of the little company in the fort.

They had water, and their guns had thus far been able to bring them food; but the salt had given out, and salt was a thing that they must have. " I will go for it," said Boone. With thirty men he started on a journey of one hundred miles through a wilderness where at any moment hundreds of Indians, well armed with British guns, might fire at them. They reached the salt springs safely. Night and day they worked, guns in hand, to boil the water and get the salt from it. For four weeks they were left alone, then they were suddenly attacked by four times their number of Indians and had to yield. They were taken to Detroit, where the others were given up for ransom; but the red men would not give up Boone for any sum. They had a plan to persuade him to live with them and become one of their chiefs. He guessed this and pretended to be satisfied. " Now we will adopt you," they said. But most people would

have preferred not to be adopted, for part of the ceremony was plucking out all his hair except the scalp-lock.

Then he was
taken to the
river and washed
to make sure that
no white blood
was left in him,
and after his face
was painted he
made a very good
chief.

The Indians
were too shrewd
to believe that
Boone would not
go home if he
had a chance;
so when he went
out to hunt, they
counted his balls

BOONE AMONG THE INDIANS

and measured his powder. They knew that
if he had no ammunition he would not attempt to run away, for without it he would
soon starve in the forest. He did save up ammunition,
however, in spite of them, for he used no more than
was absolutely necessary and cut every bullet in two.

One wise thing that Boone did when he was captured was to pretend to know nothing of the language of the Indians, though he really understood everything that they said. They talked freely before him, and he learned that they were planning to attack Boonesborough. The war-dances were held, and Boone joined in them. But one morning he went out to hunt and did not return. Five days later there was great rejoicing in the fort, for Boone had come back, though they had thought him surely dead. He was none too soon. In a little while a body of Indians marched upon the fort. " In the name of his Majesty King George of Great Britain, we summon you to surrender," they said. There were ten times as many of the enemy as there were settlers, but Boone replied, " We shall defend our fort so long as one man is alive."

Then came fierce fighting that went on day and night for nine days. One day the Americans noticed that the water of the river was becoming muddy, and they knew that the enemy were digging in from the bank to undermine the fort. They broke up this plan by digging another passage to cut the first. The Indians shot fire-arrows to try to set fire to the fort, but the Americans were too watchful to allow them to do any damage. At last the Indians gave it up and went away. Boone said quietly that they had been very industrious, for one hundred and twenty-five pounds of bullets were picked up in the fort, besides what stuck in the logs. Never again did the Indians attempt to take Boonesborough. Daniel Boone had explored the country, made a road to it, brought in settlers, and defended them.

OUTLINE

Different ways of helping in the Revolution — Daniel Boone's early home — his marriage — he hears of Kentucky — goes to see it — fights the Indians — his road-making — building a fort — a defense against the Indians — new settlers arrive — dangers from Indians — Boone goes for salt — captured and taken to Detroit — adopted by the Indians — closely watched — learns their plans — escapes — attack on the fort — the repulse — what Boone did for Kentucky.

SUGGESTIONS FOR WRITTEN WORK

Who helped the country most, — those who raised money, those who aroused interest, or those who settled in the wilderness?

Indians describe an attempt to take a fort.

Boone's daughter sees her father coming after his escape from the Indians.

MERIWETHER LEWIS AND WILLIAM CLARK

WHO SHOWED THE WAY TO THE PACIFIC

AT the close of the Revolution, the United States owned all the land from the Atlantic to the Mississippi and from Canada to Florida. France had lost

Canada, but she still held the country between the Mississippi and the Rocky Mountains. About twenty years after the war France needed money, and she sold this land to the United States at about two and a half cents an acre. The next thing was to find out what kind of country had been bought. The government asked Meriwether Lewis and William Clark, brother of George Rogers Clark, to explore it. It was thought that the best way would be to follow up the Missouri River, then to enter the Columbia River, and so get to the Pacific Ocean; but no one had any idea where the sources of the two rivers might be. The only way to learn was to go and find out.

No one knew what dangers there would be. There were stories of mountains so lofty that no man could ever climb them; of Indians more fierce and more cruel than any that had been known; but the stout-hearted company set out, not in the least frightened by all these tales. There were forty men or more in the party, the wife of the interpreter, and her baby, the youngest of American explorers.

This company was to do much more than simply to push through to the Pacific Ocean. They were to note the mountains and valleys and rivers; to draw maps showing where there were rapids or falls; to see what kinds of soil, trees, flowers, fruit, animals, and minerals there were in different parts of the country. In short, they were to keep their eyes open, and on their return to tell the government where they had been and what they had seen. One thing more they were to do, the most important of all, and that was to make friends with the Indians, to learn how they lived and what lands each tribe claimed, and especially to open the way for trading with them. It seems like going back to the days of

Champlain to read the list of what the travelers carried to give or sell to the red men. There were beads, paints, knives, mirrors, red trousers, coats made gorgeous with gilt braid, and many other things that would please the savages.

Then they set out on a journey which proved to be

two years and four months long. And such wonders as they saw! In one place the water had worn away the earth into such shapes that the explorers were sure they had come upon an ancient fort. In another was a wide river with bed and banks and falls and rapids, but not one drop of water. There were antelopes and prairie dogs and other animals which were new to them. There were buffaloes so tame that they had to be driven out of the way with sticks and stones. There were water-falls so high that the water fell part way, then broke into mist, but gathered together again and made a second fall, which seemed to come from a cloud.

There were some things to meet that were not quite so interesting as double waterfalls. There were brown bears and black bears and grizzly bears, all anxious to greet them with a hug. There were long marches over ground covered with sharp pieces of flint, and there were other marches over plains where the thorns of the prickly pear pierced their shoes as if they were only paper. Sometimes they were driven half wild with clouds of mosquitoes. " The Musquetoes were so nu-merous that I could not keep them off my gun long enough to take sight and by that means Missed," wrote Captain Clark in his journal. Captain Lewis once was separated from his men for a few hours, and in that time he met a grizzly bear, a wolverine, and three buf-falo bulls, all of which showed fight. Again he lay down

under a tree, and when he woke he found that he had
had a big rattlesnake for next-door neighbor. He nailed
a letter upon a tree for some members of the party who
were to come after him; but when they came they found
that the beavers had gnawed the tree down, carried it
away to use in their dams, and so had stolen the whole
post-office. One night the company camped on a sand-
bar in the river; but they were hardly sound asleep
before the guards cried, "Get up! Get up! Sand bar's
a-sinking!" They jumped into the boats and pulled for
the farther shore, but before they reached it the sand-
bar was out of sight. There were other disturbances
of their dreams. Another night they camped near an
island which proved to be the home of ducks and geese
and other wild fowl that quacked and hissed and made
all the noises that they knew how to make, while the
tired men rolled and tumbled and wished they had more
quiet neighbors. Another night a buffalo dashed into
their camp and ran between two rows of sleepers. And
to cap the climax, the baby explorer had the mumps and
was cutting teeth and cried all night.

Getting food was not always an easy matter. In one
place they exchanged roast meat, pork, flour, and meal for
watermelons; but they had not often so luxurious fare.
Frequently they had nothing but a little flour or meal,
and for a long while they lived on horse-flesh and dog-
flesh. Often they were glad to buy eatable roots of the

Indians. Sometimes the Indians refused to sell. On one such occasion, Captain Clark threw a port-fire match into the fire, and then took out his compass and with a bit of steel made the needle whirl round and round. The Indians were so terrified that the women hid behind the men, and the men hurried to bring him the roots that they had sullenly refused to sell. On the Fourth of July the explorers lived in luxury, for they feasted on bacon, beans, suet dumplings, and buffalo meat; but when Christmas came they had nothing but stale meat, fish, and a few roots. The Indians once cooked them some meat by laying it on pine branches under which were hot stones. More branches were put on top of the meat, then a layer of meat, then another layer of branches. Water was poured upon the mass, and three or four inches of earth spread over the whole heap. The white men did not like the flavor of pine, but they admitted that the meat was tender.

They tried to make friends with the Indians wherever they went, by giving them medals and other trinkets that they had brought. They told them about the Great Father in Washington who wished them to be his children, and who would always be kind to them. Sometimes they shared their food with the red men. One Indian ate a piece of dried squash and said it was the best thing he had ever tasted except a lump of sugar that some member of the party had given him. One tribe to whom they offered whiskey refused it. " I am surprised," said the chief, " that our father should give us a drink that would make us fools."

Talking with the Indians was not always easy. This is the way it was sometimes done. Captain Lewis or Captain Clark spoke in English; one of the men put

LEWIS AND CLARK MEETING THE INDIANS
(By courtesy of the Northern Pacific Railway)

what he had said into French; the interpreter put it into an Indian dialect that his Indian wife understood; she put it into another tongue which a young Indian in the party understood; and he translated it into the language of the tribe with whom they wished to talk. It was no wonder that whenever it was possible they avoided this roundabout method and used the language of signs. When a man wished to say, for instance, "I have been gone three nights," he had only to rest his head on his hand to suggest sleep and to hold up three fingers. He could say, "I came on horseback" by pointing to himself and then placing two fingers of his right hand astride his left wrist. To hold a blanket by two corners, shake it over the head, and unfold it, meant "I am your friend; come and sit on my blanket." If the Indian accepted the invitation, the next scene was not very agreeable; for he would wish to embrace the white man and rub his cheek, thick with red paint, on that of his new friend.

One language was understood by all, the language of gifts. A string of beads went a long way in winning friends. The red men had their fashions in beads, however; blue or white beads were very welcome, but they cared little for other colors. They were fond of dancing. One evening several hundred Indians seated themselves around the white men's camp and waited till the violin struck up and a dance took place. After an hour or two, the white men said, "Now it is your turn. Show us how you dance." The red men and women and children sprang to their feet and crowded together around an open space. A few young braves leaped into the space and carried on something that might be called a dance; but all that the rest of the company did was to sing and jump up and down in time with the music. They were as fond of games as of dancing. The most common game was one often played now by white children. A man passed a tiny piece of bone back and forth from one hand to the other, then held out both hands closed. The one who was playing against him pointed to the hand in which he thought the bone was. If he guessed right, he won the blue beads or whatever else the prize might be. If he lost, the other man won it.

SACAJAWEA, THE INDIAN WOMAN WHO GUIDED LEWIS AND CLARK

So it was that, dancing, climbing mountains, shooting rapids, killing bears and mosquitoes, dragging canoes up rivers, making friends with the Indians, eating or fast-ing, the brave explorers made their way to the source of the Missouri, a streamlet so narrow that one of the men took his stand with one foot on either bank. Three-quarters of a mile farther, they came to a creek running to the westward. This was one of the branches of the Columbia. Onward they went, and at last they stood on the shore of the Pacific. It was the rainy season. Their clothes and bedding were always wet, and they had nothing to eat but dried fish. It is no wonder that they did not feel delighted with the scenery. Captain Clark wrote in his journal that the ocean was " tempestuous and horrible."

At last they started on the long journey back to the east. There were the same dangers to go through again, but finally they came to the homes of white men ; and when they caught sight of cows feeding on the banks of the river, they all shouted with joy, the herds looked so calm and restful and homelike. When they reached the village of St. Louis, they received a hearty welcome, for all supposed that they had perished in the wilderness. These courageous, patient men had done much more than to explore a wild country. Just as Columbus had made a path across the Atlantic, so they had made a path to the Pacific. They showed the way; and the thousands who have made the western country into farms and villages and cities have only followed in the footsteps of these fearless explorers.

OUTLINE

Growth of the United States — plans for exploration — the company sets out — the aims of the explorers — goods for barter — what wonders were seen — hardships of the journey — wild animals that they met — a stolen post-office — a sinking sandbar — noisy neighbors — getting food — an Indian way of cooking — making friends with the Indians — difficulty of talking with the Indians — the sign language — gifts to the Indians — an Indian dance — Indian games — the source of the Missouri — a branch of the Columbia — the shore of the Pacific — the journey home — the welcome — what the explorers had done.

SUGGESTIONS FOR WRITTEN WORK

A boy tells why he wants to go with Lewis and Clark.

Which articles carried by the explorers for barter would be most valued by the Indians ?

The greatest hardship that the explorers had to meet.

THE LEWIS & CLARK CENTENNIAL
PORTLAND - OREGON - 1905

OLIVER HAZARD PERRY

WHO CAPTURED A BRITISH FLEET

WHEN the children born at the close of the Revolution had become men and women, another war, known as the war of 1812, broke out between England and the United States. During this war both parties were anxious to get control of Lake Erie. The American government decided to build some ships on the lake, and appointed Oliver Hazard Perry, a young man of twenty-seven, commander of the fleet. He and his younger brother set out in an open sleigh for Erie, where the vessels were to be built. Perry found that the government was not a very good builder of ships. There was no seasoned timber, no iron, no canvas, ropes, anchors, cannon, muskets, balls, or cartridges. Worst of all, there were no shipbuilders. The men to whom the order to build had been given had done as well as they could. They had sent for shipbuilders to New York and Philadelphia, a journey of four or five weeks, and in the mean time they had set house-carpenters to work.

Luckily, the young commander had taken charge of building a fleet before, and after he came there was no more delay. The shipbuilders arrived who had started some time before; trees were cut down in the forest, dragged to the shipyard, cut into beams and planks, and

made into parts of vessels, — all within twelve hours.
Men were sent in various directions to get what was
needed. They scoured the country for iron and brought
in hinges, locks, chains, old kettles, wheel-tires, bars,
and bolts from wherever they could be found. Guns
and ammunition and whatever else was needed were
hurried in. In less than two months after Perry arrived,
three gunboats were launched, and two sloops were
ready a few weeks later.

The British knew what was going on at Erie, but
Perry's guard kept close watch that no one should slip
up to the vessels in the night and set them on fire. There
was no danger from the British ships on the lake, for in
front of Erie stretched a long sand-bar which no ship
drawing more than seven feet of water could sail across.
Of course Perry's vessels must get over the bar in some
way, and Captain Barclay, the British commander, was
watching closely. "That will be slow work," he said
to himself, "and when they begin to go over the bar is
the time for me."

Unfortunately for Captain Barclay, he was invited
to dinner on the other side of the lake, and accepted the
invitation. Perry, too, had been watching. "This is the
time for me," he said, and gave the order to cross. His
flagship, the Lawrence, was the largest of the fleet. She
was brought up to the bar with a big scow on each side.
The scows were nearly filled with water, and while they

were very low in the water, blocks were piled upon them. Then the water was pumped out, and as they rose, they struck against stout beams which had been pushed into the port-holes of the Lawrence and lifted the vessel safely over the bar. The other ships came across with less trouble.

Captain Barclay had hoped to capture a ship while it was crossing, but he was in no hurry to have a general battle. He, too, was building a ship, the Detroit, and he meant to have it finished before any fighting began. Therefore he slipped away and got out of sight as fast as possible. He had not a great supply of provisions, but he waited a month for his new vessel and then sailed out, ready for a fight. Perry, too, was ready. Upon his flagship he ran up a blue flag on which in clear white letters was Lawrence's dying command, " Don't give up the ship ! "

On the Detroit the musicians played " Rule, Britannia! — Britannia, rule the waves! " A bugle was sounded. " Hurrah ! Hurrah! Hurrah ! " shouted the men on the British vessels. Then the combat began, and a fearful combat it was. The Lawrence became only a shattered hulk. " Perry has lost his flagship," thought the British, "and he will soon surrender." But Perry had no such intention. He wrapped his flag around his arm, then he and his brother, with four seamen to row them, leaped into a boat. The seamen pulled with all their

PERRY'S VICTORY ON LAKE ERIE

"If a victory is to be won, I'll win it."

might. At first the smoke hid them from their enemies; then the British caught sight of them and fired volley after volley. Two bullets went through the boy's cap, but no one was injured; and in fifteen minutes after they left the Lawrence, Perry had run up his flag on the Niagara, and, with his new flagship, was all ready for another battle. It was a short one, and then came the surrender of the British. It was the first time that England had ever lost a whole squadron, but now she surrendered one, not to an old experienced commander, but to a young man of twenty-seven who had never before even seen a naval battle.

The first thing to do was to report to the Secretary of the Navy. Perry must have enjoyed writing that report, for he had begged the secretary more than once to be sent where there was likely to be fighting, and that official had paid no attention to his request. While he was building the ships, he had almost pleaded for men. " Give me men, sir," he had said to Commodore Chauncey, " and I will gain both for you and myself honor and glory on this lake or perish in the attempt." After writing his formal report to the Secretary of the Navy, he sent off his famous note to General Harrison, which said, " We have met the enemy and they are ours."

The British had been planning to invade what was then called the Northwest Territory, that is, the land

now forming Ohio, Indiana, and Illinois; but now that
Perry had captured their fleet, he had control of Lake
Erie, and all their plans of invasion came to nothing.
It is no wonder that the whole country rang with the
praises of the young victor. Congress formally thanked
him, promoted him, and gave him a medal. Cities took
holidays, rang their bells, fired their guns, and illumi-
nated their houses in his honor. Everybody who could
make two lines rhyme set to work to write a poem
about him. Boston gave him a silver service. Other
cities gave him swords, and as for votes of thanks,
the land fairly echoed with them.

This was not the end of Perry's service by any means,
for he had much more to do for his country before the
war was over. One thing was to help defend Baltimore when the British fleet was trying its best to capture her forts. His life was short, for only seven years
after the war of 1812 began, he died in South America.
Congress sent a man-of-war to bring home his body that
it might rest in the land which he had so bravely helped
to defend.

OUTLINE

Ships to be built on Lake Erie — Perry goes to Lake Erie — the
government a poor shipbuilder — work is begun — getting iron —
setting a watch — advantage of the sand-bar — Captain Barclay's
plans — what happened when he went to dinner — he avoids a battle — the two flagships — Perry loses his flagship — he finds a new

one — the British surrender — Perry's report and note to General Harrison — value of this victory — celebration of the victory — Perry's further service —his death.

SUGGESTIONS FOR WRITTEN WORK

Perry's brother describes: — building the ships; getting the Lawrence over the bar ; the battle.

DOLLY MADISON

WHO GUARDED THE NATION'S TREASURES

"DOLLY," asked President Madison of his wife, "have you the courage to stay here till I come back to-morrow or next day ?"

"I am not afraid of anything if only you are not harmed and our army succeeds," was her reply.

"Good-by, then, take care of yourself, and if anything happens, look out for the Cabinet papers," said the President, and rode away to where the militia was gathering.

There was good reason for Mrs. Madison to be anxious about her husband and about the success of the Americans. It was now 1814; America and England had been fighting for two years. Many people thought that the President had been wrong in resorting to war. Letters had been sent him which said, "If this war does not come to an end soon, you will be poisoned." The city of Washington, too, was in great danger. Four days earlier a messenger had ridden up at full speed to say, "Fifty British ships are anchoring off the Potomac." Nearly all the men hurried to the front to try to oppose the enemy. People in Washington were carrying their property away to the country. Still the little lady at the White House did not run away. She had the public papers to guard, and she would not go.

DOLLY MADISON

Besides the papers, there was another of the nation's treasures in the house, a fine portrait of George Washington by the famous artist, Gilbert Stuart. The son of Washington's stepson came to Mrs. Madison to plan for its safety. "Whatever happens, that shall be cared for," she had promised him.

At last a note came to her from the President. "The enemy are stronger than we heard at first," it said. "They may reach the city and destroy it. Be ready to leave at a moment's warning."

Most of her friends had already gone, but her faithful servants were with her. " Bring me as many trunks as my carriage will hold," she ordered; and then she set to work to fill them with the Declaration of Independence and the other papers that were of value to the whole nation.

Night came, but there was no rest for the lady of the White House. As soon as the sun rose, she was at the windows with a spy-glass, gazing in every direction and hoping to catch a glimpse of her husband. All she could see was clouds of dust, here and there a group of soldiers wandering about, and little companies of frightened women and children, hurrying to the bridge across the Potomac. She began to hear the roar of cannon, and she knew that a battle was going on; still the President did not come. There was nothing to do but wait. It was of no use to pack the silver and other valuables, for every wagon had been seized long before, and not one was left for even the wife of the President.

At three o'clock two men, covered with dust, galloped up and cried, " You must fly, or the house will be burned over your head."

" I shall wait here for the President," was her reply.

A wagon came rumbling along. Some good friends had at last succeeded in getting it for her. She had it filled with silver and other valuables. "Take them to the Bank of Maryland," she ordered; but she said to herself, "The Bank of Maryland or the hands of the British — who knows which it will be?"

Two or three friends came to hurry her away. "The British will burn the house," they said. "They will take you prisoner; they boast that they will carry the President and his wife to England and make a show of them."

They were almost lifting her to her carriage, when she said, "Not yet. The picture of Washington shall never fall into the hands of the enemy. That must be taken away before I leave the house." This picture was in a heavy frame that was firmly screwed to the wall, and with what tools were at hand it could not be easily loosened. "Get an axe and break the frame," Mrs. Madison bade her servants. This was done, the canvas was taken from the stretcher, carefully rolled up, and sent to a safe place. Then the carriage with Mrs. Madison was driven rapidly away.

She left the house none too soon, for the British were upon the city. They broke into the White House. They stole what they could carry off with them, and set fire to the rest. They fired the navy yard, the Treasury building, the public libraries, and the new Capitol. The British Admiral Cockburn had a special spite against one of the Washington newspapers because it had printed some bitter articles about his savage burning of defenseless villages along the coast. " Burn that office," he commanded, " and be sure that all the C's are destroyed, so that the rascals cannot abuse my name any longer." It is said that he jumped down from his horse and kindled the fire with his own hand.

At night a fearful tempest swept over the city. Trees were blown down and houses were unroofed. When the storm burst, Mrs. Madison was pleading for shelter at a little tavern sixteen miles from Washington. She had seen the President, and he had told her to meet him at this place. The house was full of people who had fled from the city. " Stay out," they cried. " Your husband brought on this war, and his wife shall have no shelter in the same house with us." At last, however, they let her in. The President found his way to her later, almost exhausted; but before he had had an hour of rest, a man threw open the door, so out of breath that he could only gasp, " The British — they know you are here — fly ! " Mrs. Madison begged him to go, and finally he yielded and escaped to a little hut in the woods where he could be safe. " I will disguise myself and go to some safer place," she promised; and in the first gray of the morning she left the tavern. On the way she heard the best of news: " The British heard that reinforcements were coming and they have gone to their ships." Then she turned around and drove toward the city; but when she came to the bridge over the Potomac, it was afire. An American officer stood by. " Will you row me across the river ? " she begged, for a little boat was

THE STUART PORTRAIT OF WASHINGTON

moored to the bank. " No," he replied, " we don't let strange women into the city." In vain she pleaded, but he was firm. " Who knows what you are ? " he demanded roughly. " We have had spies enough here. How do I know but the British have sent you to burn what they left? You will not cross the river, — that is sure."

"But I am Mrs. Madison, the wife of your President," she said, and threw off her disguise.

Even then he could hardly be persuaded to row her across, but finally he yielded. Through clouds of smoke she made her way past heaps of smouldering ruins to the home of her sister, where she awaited the coming of the President.

Such were five days in the life of a " first lady of the land."

OUTLINE

The President's farewell to his wife — cause for anxiety — treasures in the White House — a warning sent to Mrs. Madison — she makes ready to leave — what she sees from the windows — a wagon is packed — she saves the portrait of Washington — behavior of the British in Washington — Mrs. Madison in the storm — the President comes to her — he hides in the woods — Mrs. Madison hears good news — difficulty in crossing the Potomac — she finds safety.

SUGGESTIONS FOR WRITTEN WORK

Mrs. Madison tells what she saw from the windows with her glass.

Saving Washington's portrait.

Mrs. Madison tells her sister of her experience in the storm.

THE STAR-SPANGLED BANNER

IN 1814, while the War of 1812 was still going on, the people of Maryland were in great trouble, for a British fleet had sailed into Chesapeake Bay. The cannon would be aimed at some town, but no one knew which. The ships sailed up one river, then came back and sailed up another, as if they had not decided where to go. The people who lived on the banks of these rivers fired alarm guns and lighted signal fires to let those who lived inland know that danger was near. The ships lingered, hesitated, then suddenly spread all sail and ran to the north up the Bay. "They will surely attack us," thought the people of Annapolis, and they crammed their household goods into wagons and carts, even into wheelbarrows, and hurried away to the country as fast as they could. But the ships sailed past Annapolis. Then there was no question which town was to be attacked; it was Baltimore.

As the fleet sailed on, General Ross, the British commander, spoke of his plans. "I shall have my winter quarters in Baltimore," he said.

"What about the American militia, general?" asked one of his officers playfully.

"Militia?" replied Ross; "I don't care a straw if it rains militia."

The fleet landed the soldiers at the mouth of the Patapsco River, and sailed up stream toward the town. The men marched up the river for five miles. They met a force of American militia, and there was a sharp fight for two or three hours; then the Americans retreated. " There will be no great trouble in taking the town in the morning," thought the leader; " and we will camp here to-night." When morning came, he found that, however it might be about taking the town, he would have some trouble in getting to it; for the Americans had dug ditches, and dragged heavy logs across the road. It took the whole day to get in sight of the place; and then they found it anything but an agreeable sight, for all along the hills above the city was a heavy line of entrenchments. There seemed to be plenty of men behind the entrenchments, and the British concluded that they would not take possession of their winter quarters at once. They thought it would be pleasanter to wait at least until after dark, when they would not be so plainly seen from the forts. " The cannon on our ships will surely silence Fort McHenry and the other forts and batteries by that time," they said.

While the soldiers were stumbling over logs and rolling into hidden ditches, the cannon on the British ships were firing as fast as possible. The river was so shallow that the men-of-war could not get within range of the town. " We will bombard the forts," they said. " They

THE BIRTH OF OUR NATION'S FLAG

The flag is being presented by Betsy Ross to Washington and Morris

will yield in a few hours, and then our troops can march up and take the city." For twenty-four hours the terrific bombardment went on.

" If Fort McHenry only stands, the city is safe," said Francis Scott Key to a friend, and they gazed anxiously through the smoke to see if the flag was still flying.

These two men were in the strangest place that could be imagined. They were in a little American vessel fast moored to the side of the British admiral's flag-ship. A Maryland doctor had been seized as a prisoner by the British, and the President had given permission for them to go out under a flag of truce to ask for his release. The British commander finally decided that the prisoner might be set free; but he had no idea of allowing the two men to go back to the city and carry any information. " Until the attack on Baltimore is ended, you and your boat must remain here," he said.

The firing went on. As long as the daylight lasted, they could catch glimpses of the stars and stripes whenever the wind swayed the clouds of smoke. When night came they could still see the banner now and then by the blaze of the cannon. A little after midnight the firing stopped. The two men paced up and down the deck, straining their eyes to see if the flag was still flying. " Can the fort have surrendered?" they questioned. " Oh, if morning would only come!"

At last the faint gray of dawn appeared. They could

see that some flag was flying, but it was too dark to tell which. More and more eagerly they gazed. It grew lighter, a sudden breath of wind caught the flag; and it floated out on the breeze. It was no English flag, it was their own stars and stripes. The fort had stood, the city was safe. Then it was that Key took from his pocket an old letter and on the back of it he wrote the poem, "The Star-Spangled Banner." The British departed, and the little American boat went back to the city. Mr. Key gave a copy of the poem to his uncle, who had been helping to defend the fort. The uncle sent it to a printer, and had it struck off on some handbills. Before the ink was dry the printer caught up one and hurried away to a restaurant, where many patriots were assembled. Waving the paper, he cried, "Listen to this!" and he read: —

"O say, can you see by the dawn's early light,
    What so proudly we hailed at the twilight's last gleaming,
Whose broad stripes and bright stars, through the perilous fight,
    O'er the ramparts we watch'd were so gallantly streaming?
And the rockets' red glare, the bombs bursting in air,
Gave proof through the night that our flag was still there.
    O say, does that star-spangled banner yet wave
    O'er the land of the free and the home of the brave?"

"Sing it! sing it!" cried the whole company. Charles Durang mounted a chair, and then for the first time "The Star-Spangled Banner" was sung. The tune was

" To Anacreon in Heaven," an air which had long been a favorite. The song was caught up at once. Halls, theatres, and private houses rang with its strains.

The fleet was out of sight even before the poem was printed. In the middle of the night the admiral had sent to the British soldiers the message, " I can do nothing more," and they had hurried on board the vessels. It was not long before they left Chesapeake Bay altogether, — perhaps with the new song ringing in their ears as they went.

OUTLINE

A British fleet in Chesapeake Bay — alarm in Annapolis — plans of General Ross — the soldiers land — a sharp fight — British plans for the following morning — marching to Annapolis — why the attack was delayed — bombarding the forts — Key watches Fort McHenry — where he and his friend were — their anxiety through the night — what they saw "by the dawn's early light" — " The Star-Spangled Banner " — when it was first sung — departure of the fleet.

SUGGESTIONS FOR WRITTEN WORK

The alarm of the people of Annapolis at the coming of the British.

When " The Star-Spangled Banner " was written.

The first singing of the song.

DAVID CROCKETT

THE TENNESSEE PIONEER

A FEW years before the War of 1812, there was a very homesick little boy in Virginia. His home was only a hut of logs in the wilderness of eastern Tennessee, but the one thing that he wanted most was to see it again. His father had hired him to a drover to help drive some cattle a journey of four hundred miles. No plan was made for his return, but the twelve-year-old boy made one for himself. He soon found that the only means of getting away from the drover was to run away. One stormy night he tramped seven miles through the snow to join a man who was going toward his home; but the man went so slowly that the impatient boy pushed on ahead and made much of the long journey alone.

This was the beginning of his adventures. From that time until he was fifteen he drove cattle, did farm work, and contrived somehow to get enough money together to buy a rifle. When he was fifteen he concluded that he ought to know something of books; so he began to go to school four days in the week, working two days for his board. In six months he learned to read a little, to write his name, and to do easy examples in addition, subtraction, division, and multiplication; and that was all the " schooling " that he ever had. When he was

eighteen his property consisted of a suit of coarse
homespun, a rifle, and a horse that he had not paid for.
The next thing that he did was to get a wife; but it did

THE MARRIAGE OF DAVID CROCKETT

not seem to occur to him until after the wedding that he
had no home for the pretty little girl of seventeen who
had married him. They looked about them, found a log

cabin that some one had left, and moved in. The bride's parents gave them two cows and two calves. A man for whom David had worked lent them fifteen dollars with which to furnish their house.

One day, three or four years later, David said to his wife, "Let us go to western Tennessee. The land here is all taken up, but there we can have four hundred acres if we build a house and plant some corn." The little wife was willing to go wherever her husband wished and they set out. She and her two little boys rode on the horse. The furs that they used for bedding, their few dishes, and their spinning wheel were put upon the backs of David's two colts; and so the family made a journey of two hundred and fifty miles through the wilderness. Then David built a log house, made a table and some three-legged stools, drove some pegs into the walls to hang their clothes on, if they happened to have any that they were not wearing, and they were at home. David was a remarkably good marksman, and they had plenty of venison and wild turkey. There was a stream at hand that was full of fish. No one need starve in such a place.

But David was restless. In two years he moved again. Then came the War of 1812. There was trouble with the Indians in Alabama, and he volunteered as a soldier. The Indians wished to be friendly, but some rascally white men had been stealing from them and had even shot some of them. At last the Indians began to pay back. They made an attack upon a fort and killed almost every one in it. The whole region was aroused. " I am going to help fight the Indians," said David to his wife.

" But what can we do if they come upon us ? " she exclaimed. " We are hundreds of miles from my friends. If anything should happen to you, we should starve."

So she pleaded, but David replied, " I ought to go. I owe it to my country. Moreover, if we do not punish them, they will kill us all." And away he went.

So it was that he became a soldier. He was a great favorite, and no wonder, for he was not only a daring fighter but a good hunter. After a little while the officers said one to another, " We may as well let Crockett do what he pleases, he always comes out right." So after that this independent soldier did just what he chose. He would slip away from the line of march and come back, perhaps with a turkey that he had shot. Even a squirrel was welcome in those hungry days, and whatever David had he was ready to share. No one could help liking him, for he was so generous and so full of fun. Wherever he went there were good times.

David was a strong man, but there came a time when he suddenly became very ill many miles from camp. As he lay under a tree, some Indians came that way. They stopped and looked at him. He had powder and bullets and a rifle, the three things that they cared for most; but, instead of taking them and walking off, they said by signs, " Sick? Eat this; " and they held a piece

CROCKETT ON THE MARCH

of melon to his lips. He felt so badly that he could not eat even that. Then one of them said, " You will die and be buried if you do not eat." Another said, " Come, I will go with you and carry your gun; " and they all went with him to the nearest house, a mile and a half away.

He was sick for several weeks, but at last he found his way home. A little later his wife and the youngest child were again on horseback, for now David was going to southern Tennessee. Other settlers came there, some thieves among them. "We must have a justice of the peace," the settlers declared. "Let's take Crockett." So the hunter became a magistrate. He had never read a page of a law book, but he had a good deal of common sense, and he did just what he thought was fair. When a man was accused of stealing anything, this new justice would say, "Catch that fellow and bring him up for trial." Then if he proved to be the thief, Crockett would order, "Tie him up and give him a whipping." By and by Crockett was made a magistrate by law, and now he was in trouble; for he was told that his warrant for arresting men must be in what he called "real writing," and he could hardly scribble his own name. He got over this difficulty by saying to the constable, "Whenever you see that a warrant is necessary, you need n't come all the way to me. Just fill one out, and if it is n't right, I'll change it." Then the justice went to work, and before long he could not only write a warrant but keep his record book.

But he was growing restless again, and soon he made another move. This time he built his cabin seven miles from the nearest neighbor. To this lonely place a man came one day and showed him a newspaper. It said that Crockett was a candidate for the legislature. "They mean that for a joke on me," said Crockett, "but I'll make them pay for it." So he set out to persuade people that he was the one they wanted to help make their laws; and when the time came to vote, David Crockett was elected.

By and by the backwoodsman and two well educated men were nominated for Congress. At a meeting Crockett spoke first and then was followed by the other two. They tried to answer each other, but said not a word about Crockett. One of these had been much annoyed while making his speech by some guinea hens, and at last had asked to have them driven away. As soon as he stopped speaking, Crockett called out, "General, you had not the politeness to allude to me in your speech. But when my little friends, the guinea hens, came up and began to holler, 'Crockett, Crockett, Crockett,' you were ungenerous enough to drive them all away." This raised a laugh. When the time came to vote, Crockett was elected; and later he set out in the old stagecoach for Washington.

Now David Crockett could write, but he had learned little more from books. He had, however, learned a good deal from people. He said before he went to the legislature, "If any one had come along and told me he was 'the government,' I should have believed him." But he had kept his ears open, he had asked questions, and, best of all, he had done a great amount of thinking, and had his own opinion on all questions of the day. General Jackson was the " big man " of his party, and

Crockett voted for whatever bills he proposed until one was brought forward that he did not think just. He voted against that one. After his term in Congress was over, he made a little speech, explaining why he had not followed the general. " Gentlemen," he said, " there was once a boy whose master told him to plow across the field to a red cow. Well, he began to plow and she began to walk; and he plowed all the forenoon after her. When the master came, he swore at him for going so crooked. ' Why, sir,' said the boy, ' you told me to plow to the red cow, and I kept after her, but she always kept moving.' "

People liked Crockett not only because he could tell funny stories and make them all laugh, but because he was so honest and truthful and brave; because he had so much common sense and was so reasonable; and because he was so kind and friendly and generous to every one. He was petted and praised wherever he went. Presents were given him, he was invited to dinners and treated with the utmost honor. Crowds came together to hear him speak, and he was always cheered and applauded.

But now a great disappointment came to the congressman. He had expected to be elected again, and perhaps some day to be made President; but the people who voted for him in the first place were friends of General Jackson, and they would not elect any one who was

against him. Crockett had seen his last days in Congress.
He went home and wrote, " Here, like the wearied bird,
let me settle down for awhile, and shut out the world."
But he was soon uneasy and restless. War was going
on with Mexico, and he mounted his horse and rode
away to help carry it on. He fought furiously, but
finally was taken prisoner. The Mexican President had
ordered that all prisoners should be put to death, so
David Crockett never returned to the little log house in
the Tennessee wilderness.

OUTLINE

The first adventure of David Crockett — his next three years —
his short school life — his property at eighteen — his marriage and
home — plans to go to western Tennessee — the journey — the
new home — trouble with the Indians — he becomes a soldier —
his independence — kindness of the Indians when he was ill —
he becomes a magistrate — how he treated thieves — his plan to
avoid writing — he becomes a candidate for the legislature and is
elected — Crockett and the guinea hens — what he learned — his
story of the red cow — why people liked him — why he was not
reëlected — he fights in Mexico — is put to death.

SUGGESTIONS FOR WRITTEN WORK

How David ran away.
The home of the Crocketts in western Tennessee.
The friendly Indians.

CHRISTOPHER CARSON

TRAPPER AND GUIDE

WHILE the War of 1812 was going on, a family in Missouri were aroused one night by a light knock at the door, and a hoarse whisper, " Indians ! " The father of the family caught up his gun, the mother dressed the children as well as she could in the darkness, and the whole family hurried to the log fort.

Kit Carson was one of these children, and this scene was among the earliest of his memories. It was an exciting life for a little boy, and he must have felt that his days were dull enough when his father apprenticed him to a saddler and hour after hour he had to sit and stitch on saddles and harnesses. He did his work well, but two years later, when he was eighteen, he had a chance to do something that he liked much better. A company were going to carry goods from eastern Missouri to the Spanish town of Santa Fé, and he went with them. He did not return with them, however, but pushed on farther into the mountains. When he was hungry, he shot a bird or a squirrel or a turkey or, perhaps, a deer. When night came, he made a little shelter of bark and boughs. In the mountains he chanced to meet a hunter who had built himself a hut and meant to spend the winter. Kit agreed to stay with him. With plenty of furs and wood, they were sure of being warm; and with their rifles there was no trouble about keeping the table well supplied. He studied Spanish with his new friend, and studied so hard that when spring came he could speak the language with ease.

In the spring Kit started to go home, but on the way he met some traders. When they found that he had been over the trail twice, they asked, " Will you turn back and be our guide?" The next question was, " Can you speak Spanish ? " Kit answered yes to both questions,

CHRISTOPHER CARSON

and they offered him large pay if he would go with them not only as guide but as interpreter. This was just what he wanted to do, so back he went to Santa Fé.

His next business was hunting and trapping. He would start off for a month or more with a horse to ride and a mule to carry the luggage. He wore trousers and hunting shirt, or tunic, of deerskin, often cut into fringe at the bottom and ornamented with embroidery of por-

cupine quills. On his feet were thick moccasins. Of
course he had a rifle, plenty of powder and bullets, and
a sharp knife stuck into a sheath at his belt. The mule
carried more ammunition, a blanket or two, iron traps,
and an extra knife and hatchet. Carson was in search of
beaver, and when he saw their dams in a stream he chose
some place near for his camp. To make his house he
drove two strong stakes into the ground and two shorter
ones back of them. On top of these stakes he laid
boughs and bark for a roof. The walls were also made
of bark. In half a day he could build this shed, open on
one side. His bed was a fur robe or a blanket spread
upon hemlock branches. There was plenty to eat in the
stream and the forest, so when the house was built he
set his beaver traps. Every morning he went to examine
them. He skinned the beavers that had been caught,
stretched the skins out to dry, and when he had as many
skins as his mule could carry, he went back to the settlement and sold them.

For several years he lived as trapper and guide. He
had all sorts of adventures. Once when he was alone in
the woods he shot an elk, but before he could load his
gun again he heard angry growls behind him. They
came from two big grizzly bears that were rushing toward him. Of course he ran for a tree, and swung himself up among the branches, but only a moment before
one bear struck a fierce blow with his paw. Unluckily,

grizzly bears can climb trees, as Kit well knew; but these two waited a minute, as if deciding which should go first. In that minute the hunter had pulled out his sharp knife, cut off a stout branch and made it into a cudgel. He knew that while a grizzly bear does not object seriously to being peppered with shot, he is very sensitive to even a scratch on the end of his nose. Therefore, when the first bear began to climb, Kit Carson gave him a tremendous blow right on his sensitive nose. The bear dropped to the ground howling and roaring. The other one tried it, but in a minute he, too, was howling with the

CARSON TREED BY A BEAR

pain in the end of his precious nose. They glared up

into the tree at the man with the cudgel. They growled at him, they snarled, and they roared; but neither of them cared to meet the stick again. At last they concluded that they would have to get their dinner somewhere else, so they trotted away together, still growling and occasionally looking back over their shoulders.

There was always danger from Indians. Kit Carson treated them fairly and kindly, but there were many other men who stole from them and shot them as if they were wild beasts. The Indians looked upon all white men as belonging to one tribe, and, therefore, if a white man had injured them, they thought it was only justice to punish any other white man whom they could catch. When the hunters made a camp, they had to keep close guard or their horses would be stolen. Once, when Kit Carson was with a party of hunters, they found one morning that the Indians had crept up in the night and carried away eighteen horses. Carson and eleven other men galloped after them, and at the end of a fifty-mile ride came upon them. It was noon, and the Indians had stopped to rest the animals. When they saw the white men, one Indian came toward them unarmed. That meant, "I want to talk with you." Kit Carson, also unarmed, went toward the Indian, and this meant, "I am ready to listen." The Indian said, "We never thought those horses were yours; we supposed they belonged to the Snake Indians, our enemies. The white men are our friends, and we should not think of injuring them." Not a word did they say about giving back the horses.

When they were through speaking, Kit Carson said, " I am glad that you are our friends. We are willing to forgive the mistake. We will take our horses and go away." But no horses were brought. He insisted, and at length they brought five of the poorest that they had stolen. " That is all," they said. " We will bring no more." Then both parties seized their rifles, and every man tried to get behind a tree. There was a long fight, but at last the Indians fled. All the red men who knew Carson liked him, and often, instead of shooting them or trying to keep them from shooting him, he acted as peacemaker among them. It happened once that the Sioux had been hunting on the land of the Comanches, and the two tribes had fought several battles. The chief of the Comanches sent to Carson and said, " Will you not come to help us and lead us against the Sioux ? " Carson went to them, but, instead of leading them to war, he persuaded the Sioux to leave the hunting ground of the Comanches, and there was no more fighting.

After sixteen years of such life, he went back to his old home in Missouri; but many of his friends were dead and the place was so changed that he soon left it and started to return to the west. On the steamboat going up the Missouri, he met Lieutenant John C. Frémont, whom the government had sent to explore the country west of Missouri. His guide had failed him, and he was glad to engage Carson.

Then Carson became a messenger. He went alone for three or four hundred miles, although he knew that the Indians were angry with the whites, and would be likely to kill even him if they could catch him. He went on two other expeditions with Frémont, and twice made the long journey to Washington with letters from him to the President. It must have seemed very strange to the hunter to be the guest of honor at dinners and receptions and to meet all the " great folk " of Washington and St. Louis; but he was so gentle and courteous that every one liked him, and he was so simple and sincere and so forgetful of himself that he could not be awkward.

After Carson went back to Santa Fé, he bought a large farm, or ranch, in New Mexico, and there he lived with his wife, a Mexican lady, and their children. He did other things besides managing his ranch. Once he spent many weeks driving a flock of more than six thousand sheep from his home to California. He could not have done this if he had not known so well in which direction to go and just where to find water and good pasture. Once he brought together eighteen of his old friends, and they went off on a trapping excursion up the South Platte River. They had not lost their skill, and they came back with a great quantity of furs.

The government appointed Carson Indian agent, and no better man could have been found. Almost all the tribes knew him, and called him "Father Kit." The good ones loved him, but the bad ones were much afraid of him; for if they attacked the white men, he was sure to punish them. Sometimes when he heard that the Indians were planning a war, he went straight to their encampment and talked with them as if they had been his children. "You have hundreds of warriors," he would say, "but the Great Father in Washington has thousands. You will kill some of his soldiers, but he has plenty more to call out, and in the end they will kill all your warriors. Why do you make him fight you? He does not want to fight. He wants to help you, and to have you help him." The Indians would almost always yield; and if all the white people had treated them as fairly and reasonably as did Kit Carson, there would have been few Indian wars.

Not long before Carson's death the story of his life was written, and the book was read to him. His doctor said afterwards: " It was wonderful to read of the stirring scenes, thrilling deeds, and narrow escapes, and then look at the quiet, modest, retiring, but dignified little man who had done so much. . . . He was one of nature's noblemen, pure, honorable, truthful, sincere."

OUTLINE

Carson's early memories — he is apprenticed to a saddler — he goes to Santa Fé — spends the winter in the wilderness — learns Spanish — he becomes a guide and interpreter — his hunter's dress and outfit — building his house — catching beavers — his adventure with the bears — why there was danger from Indians — he pursues the horse-thieves — he acts as peacemaker among the Indians — his return to Missouri — he meets Frémont and aids in his explorations — he is honored in Washington and St. Louis — buys a ranch in New Mexico — his journey with the sheep — his last beaver hunt — he becomes Indian agent — he hears the story of his life.

SUGGESTIONS FOR WRITTEN WORK

What was Carson thinking of while he stitched on saddles? Carson's life when on a beaver hunt. The bears' story of their meeting with Carson.

ABRAHAM LINCOLN

PIONEER AND PRESIDENT

ONCE upon a time a family of settlers named Lincoln lived in a log house in Indiana. It was hardly more than a shed, for it had neither floor nor windows. It had a doorway, but the only door was a curtain of bear-skins. There was one boy in the family, a little fellow of seven years named Abraham. " My son is going to have an education," the father used to say.

"He is going to cipher clear through the arithmetic."
The boy went to school for a little while, and learned to
read and write. His mother taught him what she could.
Among other things she told him about the War of 1812,
that had just come to an end, and about the hardships

THE BOYHOOD OF ABRAHAM LINCOLN

of the soldiers. "Everybody ought to be good to the
soldiers," she used to say. The child listened gravely,
and one day, when he had been fishing, he came home
empty handed because he had given his string of fish to
a soldier whom he met on the road.

When he was only eight years old his mother died,
and then the house was lonely indeed. After a time his

father married again. The stepmother loved the little boy, and did all she could to help him. He went to school only six months in his life, but he borrowed every book that he heard of in the country for fifty miles around. He used to read them aloud to his stepmother, and talk over with her what he did not understand. He was not quick to learn, but he never gave up a sentence until he had found out what it meant. Some of these books were *Robinson Crusoe*, *Pilgrim's Progress*, *Æsop's Fables*, the *Bible*, a life of Washington, and a history of the United States. One other book was a copy of the Statutes of Indiana. He read these laws over and over again until he knew almost the whole volume by heart. In this book were also the Declaration of Independence and the Constitution of the United States. He made himself some ink of roots, and cut a turkey quill into a pen. For paper he used a shingle. Then, when he was going to work in the field, he wrote a paragraph from the book on the wood, and whenever he stopped a minute to rest, he pulled out his shingle and read a little to think over when he was working.

"I should like to be a lawyer," he said to himself; but even when he was twenty-one it did not seem as if he would ever be able to carry out his wish. Indeed, he himself thought that it might be a good thing for him to become a blacksmith, because he was so tall — six feet and four inches — and so strong. His father needed help, however, for he was just moving to a new farm in Illinois, and there was much for them both to do. After building a new log house, the next thing was to cut down some of the tall walnut-trees and split them into rails for a fence. How Abraham Lincoln

THE EARLY HOME OF ABRAHAM LINCOLN

would have opened his eyes if some one had whispered what those rails would be used for thirty years later!

The next thing that the young man did was to help a man build a flatboat and float a load of goods down the Mississippi to New Orleans. On their return, he "hired out" to work in this man's store, but in a year the store was closed. Just at that time the Black Hawk Indian War broke out, and Lincoln volunteered. The

men of his company chose him captain, and he was much
pleased, though he had little notion how to drill them.
He always had his wits about him, however, and could
generally find a way out of his difficulties. One day his
company were marching across a field four abreast
when they came to a gate. The new captain had not
the slightest idea what command to give to get them
into single file so they could go through, or, as he
put it, to get them " through the gate endwise; " so he
shouted, "The company is dismissed for two minutes,
when it will fall in again on the other side of the gate."

The war lasted only a few months. Then Lincoln
and another young man bought out the village store.
Many stories are told of Lincoln as a storekeeper.
One is that by mistake he charged a man sixpence too
much and that very night walked three miles to the
man's house to return the money. He did other things
than tie up sugar and tea, for the village schoolmaster
had become his friend and was lending him books, hearing him recite, and correcting his compositions. Lincoln's partner was careless, and Lincoln himself was
perhaps too much interested in study to watch him
closely. The result was that the business failed. Then
Lincoln said to his creditors, " I mean to pay that money,
and if you will trust me, I will give you every cent that
I earn above what is enough to live on." He owed
eleven hundred dollars. He used to speak of it as the

" National Debt." Finally he paid every penny of it, and that was why his neighbors called him " Honest Abe."

Keeping store was bad for his pocketbook, but something happened one day when he was behind the counter that was very good for him. A man who was moving west with his family drove up and said, " Look here, this barrel's in the way. I 've no room in the wagon for it, and there 's nothing of much value in it. I 'll sell it for half a dollar. Will you buy it? "

To oblige the man, Lincoln bought the barrel, rolled it out of the way, and forgot all about it. Some time afterwards, he came upon it, knocked the head off, and turned it over to see what was in it. At the very bottom were Blackstone's *Commentaries*, famous law books. Lincoln opened the volumes and began to read. " The more I read, the more interested I became," he said. He determined not to be a blacksmith or a storekeeper or anything else but a lawyer; and after much hard work a lawyer he became. His studying did not stop then by any means, for he gave a certain number of hours every day to the studies that he would have taken up had he been in college. He worked hard on his cases, too. He went over the case in his own mind, thinking over all the reasons for believing that his client was in the right. Then he tried to think of everything that the opposing lawyer could say to show the man in the wrong and of what he himself could say in reply.

In one famous case of which he had charge, he defended an old neighbor who was accused of murder. One witness after another said, " I saw him commit the murder."

" What time was it? " Lincoln asked quietly.

" About eleven," they answered.

" How could you see so clearly at eleven o'clock at night? " he demanded.

" The moon was shining," they said.

" Just where was the moon and how large was it? " he asked. They told him its size and in what part of the sky it was.

Then Lincoln pulled an almanac out of his pocket and said to the court, " This is all the defense I have. This almanac declares that theré was no moon on the night of the murder." The witnesses had made up their story together, but had forgotten to see whether it agreed with the moon. The man was declared to be innocent.

Lincoln had been made a member of the state legislature and had been a congressman. In 1860 a meeting was held to nominate a Republican candidate for the presidency of the United States, and Lincoln was chosen. Of course there were all sorts of emblems and decorations used in the campaign, but the one that people looked at most was two weather-beaten fence rails trimmed with flowers and streamers and lighted tapers. Over them was a banner which said they were two of the rails cut by Abraham Lincoln thirty years before. When he was asked about them, he replied, " I don't know whether we made those rails or not; fact is, I

Copyright, 1891, by M. P. Rice
ABRAHAM LINCOLN

don't think they are a credit to the maker; but I know this, — I made rails then, and I think I could make better ones than these now."

Lincoln became President, but there must have been many days during the five years following when he wished he had no harder work than splitting rails, for the Civil War broke out. The President is commander-in-chief of the army; and Lincoln set to work to study how to carry on war. He used every spare minute to read about the subject. Then he called the military committees of Congress together and laid before them the plan that he had made. They did not follow it, but to-day people who are wise in warfare say that if it had been followed the war would have ended much sooner. One of his generals was so insolent that the members of the Cabinet were angry and indignant; but even then Lincoln did not lose his patience. "Never mind," he said, " I will hold his horse for him if he will only bring us success."

Every day crowds of people came to see the President, and almost every one wanted some favor. One wanted to be postmaster somewhere, another wanted promotion in the army, and many came to plead that he would pardon some soldier who was condemned to die for deserting or sleeping at his post. It is no wonder that the weary President said to his secretary, " I wish George Washington or some other old patriot were here to take my place for a while, so that I could have a little rest." Tired as he was, he would not send people away. Even when a man persisted in reading him a long, wearisome paper, he did not refuse to listen. "What do you think of it ?" the author demanded. "Well, for those who like that sort of thing," replied the tired man, "I should think it is just about the sort of thing they would like."

It was almost impossible for him to refuse to pardon a soldier. Perhaps he remembered that his mother had said to him when he was a little boy, "Everybody ought to be good to the soldiers." The generals objected. They begged him not to interfere, but still the President could not help writing pardons. "It rests me after a hard day's work," he said, "if I can find some good cause for saving a man's life; and I go to bed happy as I think how joyous the signing of my name will make him and his family and his friends."

One day an old man came to plead for the life of his son, a soldier who had been sentenced to death. "I am sorry I can do nothing for you," said the President, "but the crime is unpardonable. Hear what General Butler telegraphed me yesterday." And he read, "President Lincoln, I pray you not to interfere with the courts-martial of the army. You will destroy all discipline among our soldiers." Then the old man was hopeless, and he broke down completely. Lincoln could not bear to see his sorrow. Suddenly he burst out, "Butler or no Butler, here goes!" and he wrote that the boy was not to be shot without further orders from the President. "There," he said, "if your son never dies till orders come from me to shoot him, he will live to be a great deal older than Methuselah."

At last the war came to an end, but only a few days after its close the President was assassinated. The poet, Walt Whitman, expressed his own grief and that of millions of others in his poem, "My Captain." In this the "Captain" is President Lincoln, the "ship" is the Union, and the "voyage" is the cruel war that had just come to an end.

"The ship is anchor'd safe and sound, its voyage closed and done,
  From fearful trip the victor ship comes in with object won;
    Exult O shores, and ring O bells!
      But I with mournful tread,
        Walk the deck my Captain lies,
        Fallen cold and dead."

OUTLINE

Lincoln's early home — his father's plans for him — his mother's teachings — his stepmother's aid — what he read — how he studied in the field — his plans for the future — he splits rails — visits New Orleans — works in a store — becomes a soldier — how he managed a drill — his life as a storekeeper — the "National Debt" — how he decided to become a lawyer — his studying — how he prepared his cases — defending a neighbor — the exhibition of the fence-rails — Lincoln becomes President — how he made plans to carry on the war — his patience with an insolent general — his tiresome visitors — his pardons for soldiers — the assassination of the President — Walt Whitman's poem.

SUGGESTIONS FOR WRITTEN WORK

The boy Abraham Lincoln gives his fish to the soldier.

The fence-rails tell the story of their lives.

The old man whose son Lincoln pardoned tells his wife about the President.

THEODORE ROOSEVELT

AMERICAN CITIZEN

ONE day a boy of thirteen was in a stage-coach on his way to Moosehead Lake, in Maine. He was a slender, narrow-chested boy. He had asthma so severely that for years he had to " sit up when he lay down." He was so nervous and sickly that he had never been able to go to school. He had passed many such days as are thus recorded in his little diary: " I stayed in the house all day varying the day with brushing my hair, washing my hands and thinking in fact haveing a verry dull time."

But whether sick or well he could tell most fascinating stories, and he read everything that came to hand. He read the seven hundred pages of Livingstone's *Travels in Africa* when he was hardly large enough to drag the big volume around. He read Cooper's novels. He read of Daniel Boone and David Crockett; he read *Little Women* and *A Summer in Leslie Goldthwaite's*

Life, and all sorts of books for both boys and girls. He had pets of many kinds — cats, dogs, rabbits, ponies — and he was so interested in animals that he and his cousins founded what they called the " Roosevelt Museum of Natural History."

The Roosevelts lived in New York City, but their summers were usually spent in the attempt to find some place where the suffering boy might be free from asthma. Moosehead Lake had been recommended, and thither he was going. Two strong, well boys in the coach had a fine time tormenting him. His brother, who had always defended him, was not there, and he tried to fight them, one at a time. He had plenty of pluck, but no muscle, and he was mortified to find that either of them could master him as if he had been a rabbit.

The feeble, sickly boy made up his mind that if it was possible he would make himself strong, and he took lessons in boxing and wrestling and practiced gymnastics with energy day after day. At eighteen he entered Harvard. He belonged to clubs and was active in every one of them. He wrestled and boxed and ran and rowed and had the measles. He taught in a Sunday school. One of his class of boys appeared with a black eye gained in defending his sister from insult. The young teacher gave him a dollar to encourage him in well-doing, and was requested by the church authorities to give up his class. Twice every year he went to Maine on hunting trips. He was elected to the Phi Beta Kappa for his scholarship. His four years in college were strenuous.

Of course, like every other boy, he had been thinking of what he meant to do in the world. He had once decided to be a naturalist; but at that time a naturalist was generally expected to be, not a man who devoted himself to observing plants and animals, but a man who spent his days with a microscope in a laboratory. This would never do for him, and he began to read law, but soon found himself in politics.

He went in with all his might, and a year later he became a member of the New York Legislature.

PRESIDENT ROOSEVELT IN THE WHITE HOUSE

He was only twenty-three, the "baby member." He did not know how to make a speech, but a friend gave him some good advice, "Don't speak until you are sure you have something to say and know just what it is, then say it and sit down." He lived up to this counsel and, as Bill Sewall, his Maine guide, said, "Theodore was n't remarkably cautious about expressing his opinion." He became known as the " cyclone member."

There was one opponent, however, whom even cyclone speeches could not move, and that was the asthma. He longed for the wild, and soon he and his duffle-bag arrived in North Dakota. He wanted to go hunting buffalo, but guides were not interested in a "tenderfoot" with glasses. At length one was found. Then came wild life enough to satisfy even " Four-Eyes," as the ranchers called the city man. He was thrown from his horse again and again, but once he stuck on so firmly that horse and hunter rolled down a sand cliff together. He tumbled into a cactus and filled his hands with needles. He cut a gash in his forehead; but he met every adventure with such pluck that the ranchmen gave him their highest compliment and declared that he was a " plumb good sort." This was his record for three weeks. Then he bought a ranch. So it was that Theodore Roosevelt became a ranchman.

After another session of good work in the Legislature, he returned to the West. He went on hunting trips; he fought forest fires; he rode forty hours on a stretch; he worked hard, he played hard, and, when he had to, he fought hard. He heard that a man threatened to kill him. He went to the man and said quietly, " I hear that you want to shoot me. I came over to find out why." They parted good friends. To another man who had made himself unpleasant, he said sharply, " Fight now or be friends." The man stared, then said, " Make it friends."

On Roosevelt's invitation, Bill Sewall, the fearless, upright, intelligent backwoodsman, together with his wife and three-year-old daughter, also his nephew, Will Dow, and his wife, had come to share in the ranch life; and a wild, rough, hard life it was. Roosevelt broke his shoulder, but there was no doctor to help it mend. Once he just saved himself from plunging over a crumbling bank into the little Missouri. He did go over a preci-pice, but landed safe and sound in a tall pine tree. He was too busy to be killed. Three men stole his boat. Roosevelt had been made deputy sheriff, and he with Bill Sewall and Will Dow pursued them. The thieves were captured, and, with a recollection of the cactus and its needles, the deputy sheriff took away their boots. " They won't go far through this cactus country barefooted," he declared grimly.

The six men started on a three-hundred-mile journey to the nearest jail. As far as the ice permitted, they floated downstream in the boat. Then the thieves were put into a wagon, and Roosevelt, gun in hand, followed them alone, on foot. At night they slept in a cabin, but the weary deputy sheriff sat at the cabin door and watched. The following evening he deposited them safely in jail.

Roosevelt had already written a valuable history of the *Naval War of 1812,* begun while he was in college, and now, in the midst of his adventures, he was preparing for the press a volume of his hunting experiences and was writing a life of Thomas Hart Benton. He was glad to be busy, for this brave, fearless man was grieving sorely over the death of his wife and his mother. His baby daughter was in the East, and he must have thought of her whenever he looked at the little three-year-old. The coming of the two women had made the log house more cheery and comfortable, and for two years it was home to him. Sometimes he almost thought he would make the ranch his permanent home; but wise Bill Sewall said, " No, you 'll feel different by and by, and then you won't want to stay here."

The time came. The slender, delicate boy was now the strong, robust man of twenty-eight. Asthma was among the things that were forgotten. There was a " job at home," the mayoralty of the City of New York, which his friends hoped he could win. He lost the election, but he married a young lady with whom he had corresponded when he was eleven and she was eight. He bought a home at Oyster Bay, and he continued to write books. Then he became Civil Service Commissioner. Here was a chance to do good work, and he fought to have laws made to put able men into office, and not turn them out simply because a different political party had come into power. Other men had believed in Civil Service Reform, but this man brought in a new weapon, publicity. He told the whole country what he was trying to do, and in spite of themselves he interested people in his work.

New York City was struggling to reform its government, and it certainly needed reform. On the police force, for instance, a man got a position and was promoted if he had money to pay; otherwise not. Punishment was sure for the policeman who dared to be faithful and arrested a law-breaking friend of some politician. Roosevelt became Police Commissioner, and then things changed. This new variety of commissioner meant to see for himself. He roamed about the streets in the small hours of the night, until the people began to call him Haroun al Raschid. He was especially interested in the little people of the city. His own family circle had widened. " The children are just too sweet for anything," he wrote to his wife when she was away from home; and he had a tender heart for every other child. By day and by night he visited the most wretched of the tenement houses to find out why more babies should die in one district than in another; he established playgrounds; he not only put an end to paying for promotions and gave the honest policemen a fair chance, but he made all this work public, and so aroused the sympathy of the people of New York for clean rule.

Trouble arose from Spain's abuse of Cuba. President McKinley had made Roosevelt Assistant Secretary of the Navy, and Roosevelt had done his best to prepare the navy for possible war. When war came, he offered to raise a regiment of cavalry from his beloved friends in the West, and the offer was promptly accepted. These were the "Rough Riders," as some one nick-named them. Splendid backwoodsmen, college boys, Indians, men who knew more about dancing than warfare — all joined the regiment. Roosevelt did not feel prepared to command it, and

Copyright by Underwood & Underwood, N.Y.

ROOSEVELT AS A ROUGH RIDER

the command was given to Leonard Wood as colonel, while Roosevelt became Lieutenant-Colonel.

Everybody knows the bold, fearless work of the Rough Riders in Cuba. But it was a short war, and Roosevelt had hardly reached home before he was nominated Governor of New York. He and some of his Rough Riders stumped the State, and one night, two hours after midnight, he was called from his bed to be told of his election. "I am proud of being Governor," he wrote to Bill Sewall, "and am going to try to make a square and decent one." And this he did, as some who opposed him discovered. "Occasionally I talk pretty to the gentlemen," he wrote to his sister; "occasionally I thump them with a club."

A presidential election was at hand. Roosevelt's friends wanted him to run for the office of Vice-President. His enemies were more than willing; for they thought if he was elected, he would be out of the way for four years, and perhaps his career — and his opposition to them — would be ended altogether. Roosevelt hesitated. "The best thing to do is to strive to get the position in which I can do most work," he wrote, "and that position is surely the governorship." His friends, however, believed so strongly that his name would strengthen the Republican ticket that he yielded, and was elected.

The Vice-President has not much to do, and Roosevelt planned to write some books and complete his unfinished course in law. Six months later President McKinley was shot; but he was gaining and would recover, the doctors believed. Late one afternoon, the slopes of Mount Marcy were searched and signal guns were fired, for a telegram stated that the President's condition was worse, and Roosevelt was somewhere on the mountain.

He heard the guns and answered them. Then came a

wild buckboard ride of forty-five miles to the railroad. A special train stood waiting in the darkness. President McKinley was dead. A few hours later, in Buffalo, in the presence of the Cabinet and others, Roosevelt took the solemn oath that binds a President to "preserve, protect, and defend the Constitution of the United States."

President Roosevelt was hardly established in the White House before throngs of callers began to come. He was ready to listen to everybody who brought any idea that might serve the country. Men came who worked with their brains and men who worked with their muscles. "While I am here," declared the President, "the White House door shall swing open as easily for the laboring-man as for the capitalist — and no easier."

Roosevelt was ready to strike his blow in any battle for the American people. Venezuela owed money to England, Italy, and Germany, and they were about to occupy Venezuelan territory. This would threaten the famous Monroe Doctrine that European countries must not seize land in South America. England and Italy agreed to arbitrate; Germany refused. "If Germany will not within ten days agree to arbitrate," declared the President to the German ambassador, "I shall order Dewey to go to Venezuela with battleships to prevent any German landing." "But the Emperor has already refused to arbitrate," declared the ambassador, as if that ended the matter. A week later Roosevelt asked what reply had been received from the German Government. The ambassador said no reply had come; and he was terrified when the President said quietly, "I shall order Admiral Dewey to sail, not in three days, but in two." The cable was set to work, and before the two days had passed, the Emperor had agreed to arbitrate.

Roosevelt now caused Congress to forbid the railroads to grant rebates to certain customers. He searched out frauds in the post-office and in the distribution of the public lands. The digging of the Panama Canal is due to his efforts. He was determined that the words, " I am an American citizen," should protect an American anywhere on earth, and he sent a squadron at full speed to Turkey on hearing a report that the Turks had murdered the American vice-consul. An American citizen named Perdicaris had been captured by bandits of Morocco under one Raisuli, and the Sultan of that country declared that he could do nothing about it. An American warship started for Morocco, and a telegram from the White House carried the blunt demand, "We want Perdicaris alive or Raisuli dead." The Sultan promptly found a way to rescue the prisoner.

Roosevelt was reëlected. A strenuous four years followed. Among his acts was his successful mediation between the Japanese and the Russians, who were then at war. With a view to increasing the friendliness of the South American States he sent the Secretary of State on a southern tour. To show other nations the naval power of the United States he sent the American battleship fleet around the world. Best of all, he made people at home see that the laws must be obeyed.

WITH THE RUSSO-JAPANESE PEACE DELEGATES ON BOARD THE PRESIDENTIAL YACHT MAYFLOWER, AUGUST 5, 1905.

Left to right — M. Witte, Baron Rosen, President Roosevelt, Baron Komura, Minister Takahira.

At the end of his term he went on a trip to hunt for big game in Africa and get specimens for the National Museum. He succeeded in doing this, but he did not succeed in "slipping quietly through Europe as a private citizen," for the whole Continent was eager to see him and do him honor. He was invited from country to country. In Paris he lectured at the famous Sorbonne, and in Norway he spoke urgently for a league of nations with a sufficient force to back up its decisions. The German Emperor invited him — the first time such an invitation had been given to a private citizen—to review the troop maneuvers. In London, where numerous royalties had assembled for the funeral of King Edward VII, so many kings came to call on him that he was half frantic to find time for writing necessary letters. All Europe had been expecting to find him a great man, and it found him even greater than it had expected.

In 1913 Roosevelt took a trip to South America, hunting, exploring, and almost dying of fever. Only three months after his return, Germany made her march into Belgium. Then came the sinking of the Lusitania. With all the power that was in him Roosevelt strove to induce the Government not to trust in treaties, but to prepare for what might come. When at length the German ambassador was given his passports, Roosevelt offered to raise a division of volunteers to go to France. Indeed, 200,000 had already asked to join such a division. He was refused. "Personally, I find this

Copyright by W. S. Rice.

A FAMILY GROUP

Roosevelt, Mrs. Archibald B. Roosevelt, Mrs. Roosevelt, Mrs. Richard Derby (Ethel Roosevelt), and Three Grandchildren.

a very exclusive war," he said grimly to a friend. His four sons joined the colors, much to the pride of their father. " What should you have done if you had been President at the beginning of the war ? " he was asked. " Notified the German Government that in the event of the violation of Belgian soil, the United States would call a *posse comitatus* [that is, all able fighting men] of the nation to intervene by force if need be," was his reply.

Roosevelt was not permitted to go to France, but he fought at home, fought for action, for promptness, for principle rather than policy, for straightforward Americanism. Even when severe illness attacked him, he wrote speeches, letters, and addresses, working to the last moment.

So lived and died the man whom ex-President Taft called " the most commanding, the most original, the most interesting, and the most brilliant personality in American public life since Lincoln." Even stronger praise than this he sounded in the words, " But over and above everything, Theodore Roosevelt was a deeply patriotic American."

OUTLINE

Roosevelt's health as a boy was not robust — his habit of reading — how Roosevelt built a strong body — his love of nature — the " baby member " of the New York Legislature — ranching in the West — Roosevelt becomes an author — the reform of gov-

ernment in New York City — the " Rough Riders " — Roosevelt
succeeds to the Presidency — the rights of South America — the
protection of American citizens — Roosevelt mediates between
Russia and Japan — Roosevelt's trips to Africa and to South
America — Roosevelt and the Great War.

SUGGESTIONS FOR WRITTEN WORK

The boy Roosevelt tells about three favorite books.
How Roosevelt made friends among the men of the West.
What the Rough Riders did in Cuba.
Roosevelt's travels in South America.

American Hero Stories-Afterword

by Adam Starchild

Children today are starved for the image of real heroes. Celebrities are not the same thing as heroes. Heroes existed way before celebrities ever did, even though celebrities now outshine heroes in children's consciousness.

Worshiping celebrities leaves children with a distinctly empty feeling - it doesn't teach that they'll have to make sacrifices if they want to achieve anything worthwhile. No - talents become celebrities all the time. The result is that people don't seem to care about achievement or talent -fame is the only objective.

What is a hero? Despite immense differences in cultures, heroes around the world generally share a number of traits that instruct and inspire people. A hero does something worth talking about, but a hero goes beyond mere fame or celebrity. The hero lives a life worthy of imitation. If they serve only their own fame, they may be celebrities but not heroes. Heroes are catalysts for change. They create new possibilities. They have a vision, and the skill and charm to implement their vision.

Heroes may also be fictional. Children may identify with a character because of the values projected. People tend to grow to be like the people that they admire, but if a child never has any heroes what images will he copy? Adults need heroes too, but the need is even more urgent for children because they don't know how to think abstractly. But they can imagine what their hero would do in the circumstances, and it gives them a useful reference point to build abstract thinking skills.

Good reading selections can help your children find their own heroes - to provide the emotional experience of admiring a figure they can look up to. Through the wide variety of reading experiences and choices of heroes, your children will find those models that best suit them.

It is important that children become familiar with worthy examples - both real and fictional - that they can emulate.

This does not mean that everything they read needs to be populated with heroes. Children will turn away from fictional villains they don't like. It is important to avoid children's stories in which the hero commits and gets away with evil actions. Don't assume that because a story is traditional it is automatically the literature you want your child to read. It is easy to think "that's o.k., it's a traditional children's story and I know it isn't dirty" without giving a moment's thought to the other messages that the story might be subconsciously conveying to your child.

Goldilocks and the Three Bears is certainly a traditional story, and most parents buy the book almost automatically, without a thought to the message. Goldilocks is lost and frightened, goes to a house and knocks, but no one is home. But that doesn't justify the crimes that follow. Yes, crimes! Breaking and entering, petty vandalism and theft - even the nerve to go to sleep in a bed which doesn't belong to her either.

Is this really what you intended to teach your child - that if you get lost it is alright to break into anybody's house and use their property? The story may be traditional, but these aren't the values you want to be teaching. It is so easy to assume that a well known book is okay, and select it for your child without even being aware of the subtle messages that it conveys - messages that may be having far more influence on your child than you realize. After all, aren't you the one that told your child that this was a good book - or read the story aloud? As your child is exposed to these traditional stories, you will want to take the time to explain the lessons in them. Without this guidance you may be unknowingly confusing the child. A child can also become confused when the villains in the story are likeable people who do evil.

Visible heroes today may be a bit harder to find and less dramatic, which is all the more reason to help your children start with the clear cut fictional heroes and then gradually transfer those learned ideals to the real world around them. There is no better place for a child to start than well-selected stories and novels where the hero has ability and integrity - somebody who accomplishes an important, positive job.

All children start life with the same empty brain cells. What the adults around them put into those minds determines the resulting personalities. Stories - whether heard or read - are some of the most fundamental influences on a child.

One writer whose books are highly suitable for all ages is Robert Heinlein. He uses a science fiction format to deliver important messages, and it is often easier for a child to receive and understand the message when the setting is entirely unfamiliar and the characters and events can therefore be seen more clearly. For an older child you might want to start with The Past Through Tomorrow a collection of his shorter stories. This lets the child break the reading into distinct units. For younger children look for Podkayne of Mars, Between Planets, or Have Spacesuit Will Travel.

If your child likes westerns, try some of the books by Louis Lamour.

For preschoolers, any Dr. Seuss books. They may not be obvious as sources of heroes from an adult viewpoint, but from a small child's viewpoint they have characters that are easy to remember.

For the whole family, try The Fire Hunter by Jim Kjelgaard or Girl Who Owned a City by O. T. Nelson. And Heinlein's The Rolling Stones or Farmer in the Sky. Both are strong family books about future pioneers who have to solve problems for themselves. These heroes had to make themselves intelligent and capable to make a new, better life for themselves.

Don't dismiss heroes just because they are fictional. The power of creative imagination is one that is critically important to develop in children. When they learn to imagine with confidence and pleasure things they can't actually see, it is the first step towards conceptualization and abstract thinking - important skills for handling adult challenges.

About the Author (afterword)

Adam Starchild is the author of several dozen books, and hundreds of magazine articles, primarily on business and finance.

His personal website is at: http://www.adamstarchild.com